How to design and deliver Enhanced Modules

How to design and deliver Enhanced Modules

A case study approach

By Diana Medlicott

Open University Press

Open University Press
McGraw-Hill Education
McGraw-Hill House
Shoppenhangers Road
Maidenhead
Berkshire
England
SL6 2QL

email: enquiries@openup.co.uk
world wide web: www.openup.co.uk

and Two Penn Plaza, New York, NY 10121-2289, USA

First published 2009

A catalogue record of this book is available from the British Library

ISBN-13: 978-0-33-523397-7 (pb) 978-0-33-523396-0 (hb)
ISBN-10: 0-33-523397-X (pb) 0-33-523396-1 (hb)

Library of Congress Cataloguing-in-Publication Data
CIP data applied for

Typeset by RefineCatch Limited, Bungay, Suffolk
Printed in the UK by Bell and Bain Ltd, Glasgow.

Fictitious names of companies, products, people, characters and/or
data that may be used herein (in case studies or in examples) are not
intended to represent any real individual, company, product or event.

Mixed Sources
Product group from well-managed
forests and other controlled sources
www.fsc.org Cert no. TT-COC-002769
© 1996 Forest Stewardship Council
FSC

The McGraw·Hill Companies

For all students and teachers who learn from each other

Contents

List of tables

Preface

This book came to be written because, in consulting students about their learning experiences and their perceived needs, I was confronted very forcefully with two home truths: first, that students in a mass education system need a lot more targeted teaching, learning and assessment support than is generally provided, coupled with personalized encouragement; second, lecturers and tutors in higher education aren't always really aware of this need, and, even when they are, they do not necessarily see how to build this into their teaching.

These realizations prompted me to design and deliver the Enhanced Module, and analyse its effects through action research. Enhancement means that all the normal activities in a module – lectures, seminars, tutorials, attendance monitoring, assessments and feedback – are enhanced with extras that are designed to facilitate understanding and encourage student learning. You will discover what these enhancements are over the next few chapters, but in summary it can be said that they are rooted in care and empathy for the plight of the diverse student body entering mass higher education in the twenty-first century. The book shows that, with appropriate support, students actually enjoy assessments, take notice of feedback, and discover the self-confidence and motivation that are necessary to begin the journey towards independent learning.

I have delivered my version of the Enhanced Module for four years now, and I have evaluated it each time by researching student attitudes before the module and their responses after they have experienced it. The evidence of that evaluation has been invaluable. It has shown what works and how appropriate support can transform students in positive ways. It has also meant that, in response to the student voice, I have been able to change and develop the module each time. The process of enhancement, then, is not something static: it is a fluid process, responsive to students' needs and based on the evidence of what works with students.

This book draws on that evaluation, providing evidence as to what students have liked, what they have found helpful and what they have disliked. You will find a description of a simple method of evaluation for your own modules in Chapter 16.

Of course, it is unlikely that you can just deliver the Enhanced Module with the exact form and structure that I used. You know your students best, and you are the expert with regard to their learning experience in your particular discipline. Additionally, as I did, you must work within resource limitations, timetable constraints and all the other barriers to radical change. This is not the ideal form of a module, but it is what was possible within the prevailing circumstances. But I hope you will find the principles useful and can draw upon the ways these have been put into practice.

There are many books about teaching and learning in higher education that deliver advice grounded in a diverse range of theories of education, and some of them are extremely valuable. This is not that kind of book. Although theories, particularly of student-centred learning, hover in the background like Banquo's ghost, this is essentially a practical book, for practitioners to use. It is an account of what we did, why we did it, and the effects upon our students. You will find suggestions as to other literature that also has this practical focus, so that you can follow up themes in greater detail. What I wanted to produce was a book that would be immediately useful to lecturers, tutors and teachers who want to get going on delivering exciting teaching and learning based on principles of quality. I have not assumed any prior theoretical knowledge on the part of the reader in connection with the recent progressive development of a mass higher education system.

I have just referred, rather strangely you might think, to 'lecturers, tutors and teachers'. I am uncomfortable with the job title 'university lecturer', which is the preferred term in the UK, because it implies a teacher-centred approach to learning that I do not endorse. In other countries, other terms are used. This book will use the terms lecturers, tutors and teachers interchangeably.

Acknowledgements

I owe a huge debt of gratitude to my colleague Dr Ken Smith, who was my co-teacher on the Enhanced Module. He was unfailingly supportive of my overall design, and a true 'critical friend'. He was absolutely tireless in co-delivering the module and often suggested fruitful refinements to our practice. I could not have done the action research without him, and I cannot imagine a better colleague on such a project.

I also want to thank Buckinghamshire New University for giving me the resources to carry out the action research, and in particular to Professor Bryan Mogford, Pauline Mcleman and Professor Patrick Smith for their staunch support during the early stages of the project.

I am grateful to Dr Oliver Medlicott and Flora Medlicott for their stimulating conversations about teaching, and helpful suggestions from their own practice that contributed to the ethos of this book.

Finally, I want to thank my partner Richard Yaxley for his loving encouragement during the writing of this book. When the Andalucian sunshine threatened to distract me and lure me into the mountains and olive groves, he kept me writing, and made me focus on my deadline.

Introduction

This is a book that happens to have been conceived in the UK but is relevant to higher education anywhere in the world. The contexts in which it came to be written are those of increasing educational opportunity and changing student needs, and these contexts are certainly not confined to the UK. All over the world, there has been an increasing clamour by governments, employers and students themselves to improve the quality of teaching and learning in higher education. There is a greater emphasis than ever before on transferable skills and on learning that has a closer relationship with employability.

In the UK, the nature of educational opportunity changed quite dramatically when the Labour Government came to power in 1997. Political concern was voiced about the deep and entrenched educational divide between those young people who could be described as 'advantaged' and those for whom higher education was not an option. This was a fault line that cut right through every aspect of life, so that the probable educational trajectory of young people living in the UK could often be read from their postcodes.

The principle of widening the participation and take-up of further and higher education opportunities across all social, economic and cultural divides has resulted in the proactive encouragement of those who would previously have been excluded from or disadvantaged in their pursuit of education. In political terms, widening participation is a changing context. By 2003, the UK Government target for participation in higher education of those aged 18–30 was 50%.

The widening of access to higher education has naturally resulted in a re-examination of what constitutes good-quality teaching and learning (see Biggs 2003). First of all, in order to be good, teaching must be effective. Within the context of quite rapidly widening participation, there has been a realization, not always immediate enough and not always acted on, that teaching and learning can be effective only if they are *appropriate* for a student body that is immensely *diverse* in terms of age, qualification, educational experience, social class, familial background, culture, attitude, race, ethnicity and motivation.

Diversity is a deep and chameleon-like concept, for it does not only apply to the student profile in the twenty-first century. Staff profiles, particularly in the post-1992 institutions, are much more diverse than they used to be, with many more practitioners drawn back into the academic world through the expansion of foundation degrees, vocational degrees and practice-based courses. Staff vary enormously in how they position themselves with regard to teaching, with some regarding it as their core activity, while others view it as subordinate to their primary role as researchers.

The portfolio of qualifications that enables students to enter higher education is increasingly more diverse than the old system of points based on the number of A-levels obtained. Speaking generally, it is probably fair to say that A-levels sometimes used to be mapped implicitly onto subsequent degree curricula and, in turn, degrees were delivered with implicit or explicit assumptions about student readiness because of their prior experience at A-level. The advantages of this complementarity ended as soon as it became clear that A-levels themselves were increasingly diverse in terms of structure and content, and that A-levels were only one of a number of ways in which students could qualify to enter higher education.

It is also the case now that there has been increasing diversity in the portfolio of courses offered, some of which are so rarefied that students will not have been able to study previously in those particular areas. On very many courses, some students who may have previous experience of the content of their chosen subject area will be studying alongside those who may never have studied it at all. If first-year cohorts present the kind of diversity I have outlined, it is extremely challenging for staff, who may feel that it is their task to 'feed' their students with curriculum content that will somehow bring them all to some kind of common starting line for the advanced study of their chosen subject.

To lose the psychological comfort of some sort of assumed fit between A-level study and the first year of a degree programme has not been easy for lecturers and teachers in higher education who were themselves educated in the traditional and less flexible system. The old assumptions are no longer valid (if indeed they ever were) and, faced with a roomful of first-level students, it is extremely difficult to find a bedrock of common ground in terms of prior knowledge, skills and experience. Where, then, is the starting line? And the starting line for what? What is it that we aim to do in offering higher education to such a diverse body of students?

The challenges brought out by increasing diversity in our students has been exciting, but it has not always felt comfortable for teaching staff in universities, particularly when the resources required to bring about the necessary transformation in teaching and learning have not been provided. As a result of this and other factors, student withdrawal rates have risen and the authorities have cast around for someone to blame. Wriggling on the hook of 'too much change, too quickly', theories have evolved that will locate the problem in the quality of the student intake, rather than in the startling lack of resources and support afforded to staff so that they can radically transform their teaching.

However, it has never seemed helpful to me to posit that so-called 'non-traditional' students arrive without the mental furniture and cultural capital that will set them up for success, and offer that as an explanation for their subsequent struggle and their high withdrawal rates. If indeed students do arrive without such advantages, it is the responsibility of the institution to provide them. To put it succinctly, high withdrawal rates are one indication of universities failing the *appropriateness* test. The teaching they provide is just not appropriate.

Discussion of the issues of *appropriateness* and *diversity* has frequently coalesced around the concept of *enhancement*:

> Programme Design is a creative, and often, innovative activity. The processes used by institutions to approve, monitor and review academic programmes should foster creativity and encourage *a culture of continuous enhancement* of provision.
>
> (QAA 2006b: section 7: 5, my emphasis)

The 'quality agenda' is now a formidable presence in higher education, but it is often a rather glib presence in formal documentation, or referred to superficially in endless committees. Within the context of this book, I would like to suggest that quality in higher education has three elements: good and effective teaching, measuring and evaluating that teaching, and, finally, disseminating that good practice. I want to explore these three quality elements very briefly, insofar as they bear upon the rationale of this book.

Good and effective teaching in higher education has of course always been important, and the following quotation shows that the aims of good teaching as they were construed in 1992 are still relevant today:

> ... the development of students' intellectual and imaginative powers; their understanding and judgement; their problem-solving skills; their ability to communicate; their ability to see relationships within what they have learned and to perceive their field of study in a broader perspective. The programme must aim to stimulate an enquiring, analytical and creative approach, encouraging independent judgement and critical self-awareness.
>
> (CNAA, in Gibbs 1992: 1)

Nowadays, however, the second quality element – measuring and evaluating effectiveness – is an important companion of good teaching, because of diversity in all its forms. Student perceptions are one vital and integral part of the process of measuring and evaluating good teaching, and this book is built around the evidence of student perceptions and achievements.

The third element of quality in higher education is dissemination. In disseminating this model of an enhanced module, evaluated from the student perspective, this book does not presume to teach lecturers how to teach. There are some excellent books on how to teach in higher education and, where they relate to aspects of this book, you will find them listed in the References and Bibliography. What I do presume to suggest is that stories like this one – of what we did, why we did it and what the results were – are worth disseminating, and we all need to share more of these stories.

Another point I would like to stress at the outset is that, when we are trying to deliver enhanced teaching, learning and assessment, it is easy to get overwhelmed. So although in this book I am going to try to avoid sounding too preachy, here is my advice on how to avoid that feeling of the waters closing over your head.

Remember that enhanced modules are not born: they evolve. You will find some examples in this book where I point out that, on the basis of student perceptions, we got better at particular aspects of design and delivery. And if you are not to feel hopelessly overwhelmed, it is important to remember that your job is, along with your colleagues, to offer the conditions of possibility for *development* of student understanding and intellectual powers. It is *not* your job to ensure that all students achieve them at the highest possible level. Your students will differ enormously in terms of their motivation, aptitude and levels of application, but if you offer and share with them a quality learning experience that embodies a vision of development, you will be serving them well.

In terms of your own professional development, you are probably already finding that it is as satisfying to facilitate the journey of the weakest students as that of the most able, and frequently you will see that it is indeed the weaker students who have travelled the furthest. So at the same time as having an overall vision of quality in respect of your own planning, teaching design and delivery, remember that the significant thing for each of your students is their own learning journey, and each journey will vary enormously in terms of distance, depth and sophistication.

This book is not about designing a whole programme. It is about the nuts and bolts of programmes – the modules themselves – and tells you the story of how we designed, delivered and evaluated a module with an inbuilt culture of continuous enhancement. I am not suggesting that every module should be like this, but I am suggesting that, in every programme, there should be one module at the first and second levels that sets out explicitly to deliver a continuously enhanced provision, and that it is appropriately resourced. How that module fits into the overall programme is a question for the team whose role it is to deal with the initiation, approval, monitoring and review of academic programmes in your institution.

Naturally, one module can go only some of the way towards meeting these aims, but if you sit down with your colleagues and try to think your way through a shared vision of quality, it will act as a useful framework to the activities you design, the skills you decide to focus on and the overall quality of what you deliver. It will also keep you going through bad times, and prevent you feeling hopelessly discouraged.

It goes without saying that finding your way towards a vision of quality is best undertaken with your colleagues, using the structural arrangements in place at your institution to ensure excellence and monitor quality. As early as possible in your career, you are advised to familiarize yourself with the due processes so that your input and influence can be as significant as you would like. Hopefully, you will all sign up to a quality framework and vision for the programmes delivered by your team. A division of labour can then be agreed, so that individual modules aim to deliver on specific aspects of the shared vision.

However, you may work in an institution where such fruitful collusion with your colleagues is not possible, and where, for some reason, you do not have access to the arrangements that are supposed to secure a quality framework for the programmes on which you teach. In that case, you can still set yourself a modest and realistic set of aims for your own practice. Our aims, with regard to our teaching practice on the Enhanced Module, were as follows:

- to plan and structure our students' learning
- to motivate our students, and maximize their participation, self-esteem and confidence
- to communicate our expectations clearly
- to deliver what we promised with enthusiasm and commitment
- to build strong empathetic professional relationships with our students
- to encourage each student journey towards independent learning and critical thinking.

I hope that the module model outlined in this book will give you a template through which you can be effective in the six ways described above.

How to use this book

You may be new to teaching in further and higher education, and looking for some ideas so you can begin to design the modules you are to teach. You may have been given some modules to teach and you are wondering how to adapt them to suit your own approach. You may just be looking for ideas to freshen up a module that you have been running for some time, or you may be looking to set up a module that will engage students more wholeheartedly. Your institution may be experiencing worrying levels of student withdrawal in the early stages, and you may be wondering if you can improve retention in your curriculum area. You may just be looking to beef up one particular aspect, such as your seminars, in an otherwise successful module, and would appreciate some new ideas, in which case you may find it useful to read the relevant design chapter and then turn immediately to Part 2 of the book to see how that aspect was delivered.

Whatever your motivation, you may find it helpful to know how this book came to be written, and how the Enhanced Module came to be designed in the way that it was. You may also be reassured to know that that design has been built upon evidence of student needs, and it has been tried, tested and evaluated.

The foundations for this book come from a piece of action research undertaken over a four-year period in a higher education institution in southern England that has been active in the widening participation agenda, that admits a high proportion of so-called non-traditional students, and that, like other similar institutions, has concerns about active student participation, progression and retention.

The methodology of the action research was straightforward, with the time-honoured characteristic of the teacher as researcher (Stenhouse 1975). Student perceptions were systematically gathered in relation to their needs as they entered higher education, and these perceptions were evaluated and used to formulate some research questions. The strategy chosen to address these questions was an Enhanced Module directly aimed, through its design and delivery, at addressing the problems that had been uncovered by enquiry into perceptions of the student learning experience.

Once the module was designed, and immediately prior to its delivery to a cohort of students, further research was done in the shape of enquiry into student perceptions in that cohort. Then the Enhanced Module was delivered to them, and after they had experienced it, there was an enquiry into the effects of it. The results were evaluated and compared with the evaluation prior to the strategy intervention. The final stage was to maintain, expand or modify future practice in line with what had been discovered. This cycle of action research, looking at perceptions before and after the module, was conducted four times in all, with successive cohorts of students.

Enhancing the first level of experience is a common theme both in the context of widening participation and in the specific literature on supporting student retention (Sellers and Van der Velden 2003), and the focus in this project was on identifying some perceived deficits in the first-level student experience, and then on designing enhanced provision, in the form of an Enhanced Module, that would meet those gaps. Before and after experiencing the Enhanced Module, the methods used to elicit student expectations and experiences were questionnaires and focus groups. The evaluations of the four sets of data were conducted by the same person in the same way. So the methods and recommendations in this book are evidence based, in that they have been tried, and their effects evaluated, on four successive cohorts of students, each numbering about 80.

The Enhanced Module was run four times: twice in a one-semester cycle and twice in a year-long cycle. You will see boxes inset in some of the chapters on delivery, beside each aspect of the module, which tell you how the students themselves experienced a particular feature. Interestingly, although the cohorts of students were specializing in the full range of several social science disciplines, and the numbers from each discipline varied from year to year, their overall responses were remarkably consistent over the four years. So the figures in the boxes refer to an average of all cycles, unless I specifically refer to one particular cycle.

I will indicate the content of some of the assessment tasks and seminar activities, where this is helpful in order to explain our purposes. Some of these tasks are adaptable for first-level study in a range of disciplines, and you will be able to modify the content in order to suit your own academic discipline.

In choosing our content, our central goals were to maximize student engagement with the discipline, and facilitate understanding. This could be construed as slightly at odds with the traditional convention in higher education, whereby content has so often been prioritized, possibly even at the expense of understanding and engagement.

Our approach of prioritizing understanding and engagement did, at times, involve us in building an activity around a theme that is not theoretically central to our discipline, but has intrinsic fascination for the students. For example, serial killing is not a central theoretical topic in our discipline of criminology because it is statistically rare and without a solid body of serious literature on etiology. But it is central to the sensibilities of twenty first century students, and building an activity around it is a sure-fire way of ensuring enthusiastic student participation. The topic can be used as a vehicle for promoting understanding of some key concepts, and at the same time a distinction can be made between topics that fascinate us for emotive and cultural reasons, and those that engage us for their scientific value.

Part 1

Designing the Enhanced Module

The Enhanced Module is an attempt to tackle the challenge of how to provide a positive learning environment *strategically*, *culturally* and *pragmatically*. In this first part of the book, the *strategic* design of attendance support, assessment, feedback and support for the whole student learning experience is presented as an overall package. At the same time, I hope to make it clear that there is a commitment to fostering a *culture* of encouragement and support, and, as far as possible, building this into the module design. The *pragmatic* business of delivering this package, of living up to the demanding cultural expectations we have set for ourselves and attempting solutions to the problems that are encountered, are held over until the second part of the book.

Of course, this separation between 'design' and 'delivery' is a little artificial, because the module was very much a process of evolution over four years. It is the case that we began with a design, and with our design principles, and necessarily we had to have these validated by the appropriate authorities before we could begin delivery for the first time.

But once the module began to be delivered, the evaluation of that delivery then fed back into the design, and so on, on a continuous basis. So 'design' and 'delivery' became part of a large feedback loop. This book recounts the design reached after delivering and evaluating the module four times. The separation of 'design' from 'delivery' is a useful analytical device, which makes the story of this module more accessible for the reader, and, it is hoped, more useful in designing and delivering similarly enhanced modules.

The design section in this first part of the book begins with a chapter on identifying who the module is aimed at, and what those doing the module will need, in order to succeed. This chapter is very much informed by the pre-design research aimed at eliciting student perceptions of what they feel they need. Chapter 2 builds on these perceptions to lay down some fundamental principles for the module as a whole – principles that will make for a good-quality teaching and learning experience.

In Chapter 3, the design of an attendance support package is discussed. Insufficient attention has been paid to problems of student attendance, and how to support it. The rationale for tackling this important topic early in the book is fairly obvious: you can design the best learning experience in the world, but it is not much use if no one shows up. Our attendance support policy was built around student perceptions, and focused on threading that support through curriculum and assessment.

Chapter 4 explains the design of our package of support for learning and assessment, and how we designed opportunities for feedback, following assessment, into the structure of the module. Tackling assessment support, including feedback, prior to the design of the assessments themselves is a deliberate choice. Only when support and feedback are structurally in place can decisions be made about how much assessment to provide and what that assessment should be. Chapter 5 goes into some detail about how opportunities for feedback were designed into the module from the start, while Chapter 6 explains the design of our assessment and our strategic reasons for designing it in the way we did. Chapters 7 and 8 cover, respectively, the design of seminars and lectures that support learning and facilitate understanding.

In the second part of the book, the delivery aspects of attendance support, supported learning, feedback, assessments, seminars and lectures are covered in Chapters 9 to 14, after which there are two important additional chapters and a conclusion. Chapter 15 deals with the issue of encouraging self-awareness in students, the importance of enjoyment in learning, and how students can be encouraged to reflect upon their learning. One of the pieces of assessment required them to reflect on the feedback they have received, and some of this material is quoted in this chapter in order to demonstrate the perceptions of students in relation to their learning experiences on the module. Chapter 16 summarizes the straightforward methods we used to evaluate the student experience on this module, and assesses how well we met our initial aims. Some brief examples of our commitment to a culture of continuous enhancement are included, showing how constructive criticism by students has been incorporated into changes in design and delivery. Finally, the conclusion presented in Chapter 17 identifies briefly just what has been achieved by the Enhanced Module, and makes some recommendations in terms of the provision of enhanced teaching and learning at the first and second levels of study.

1

Who are my students?

Introduction

In this chapter, we address the important issue of who our students are, so that we can begin the task of providing them with what they need in order to enjoy a good learning experience. I outline two methods of simple enquiry for finding out who our students are – one qualitative and one quantitative. I go in to some detail about the results of my qualitative enquiry, because it proved such a rich medium for eliciting students' perceptions of what they needed, and produced some common themes around which the foundational principles of the Enhanced Module could subsequently be designed. The conclusion to this chapter outlines the continuous method by which our module could be evaluated, so that we could remain in touch with who our students are and what their learning needs are.

Finding out about our students

Our starting point, before beginning the design and planning of the module structure, was to ask the following fundamental questions:

- Who are our students?
- What do they need in order to succeed?

To answer the first question, it was necessary to confront and lay to rest a somewhat unhelpful model of who our students are – or, rather, who they are not. Research has been carried out into staff perceptions of the factors relating to students failing to progress and 'dropping out' of higher education. It suggests that the tendency is for staff to explain the problem by focusing on the qualities and characteristics of the students themselves, rather than on factors relating to the design of the curriculum or the style of teaching (Taylor and Bedford 2004). Emphasis is on what students bring or fail to bring with them to college and university, rather than on what is provided for them when they get there. What they bring with them is therefore likely to be interpreted in terms of a deficit model, consisting of less than desirable levels of preparedness, motivation and ability. Sometimes there seems to be a predominating assumption that so-called 'non-traditional students', particularly those who are the first generation of their family to go on to higher education, are lacking the mental furniture and cultural background that so-called 'traditional' students possessed, and that set them up for success.

It is not really surprising if lecturers in higher education have been sensitized to this deficit model, because the language of education often seems incredibly backward-looking. There is a constant stress on the difference in contemporary and so-called 'non-traditional' students from the 'traditional' students of yesteryear. Was there ever a time when students all had three good A-levels, and were traditional clones, with similarly satisfactory aptitudes, levels of motivation and study habits? The answer is almost certainly no, but in any case this is a supremely irrelevant question. We have to work with what we get, in terms of the students we recruit, and we are responsible for putting in place the most effective teaching, learning and assessment strategies, so that the students we have recruited will succeed. If our curriculum and our strategies are aimed, even obliquely, at some idealized notion of the 'traditional' student of yesteryear, then we are clearly failing the students of today.

In relation to the two questions with which I began this chapter, I was fortunate enough to be given the resources to do some groundwork research in my institution, which enabled me to get to grips with the needs of our students in a more focused way. You will find a brief account of how I went about this below, and how it informed the design of the Enhanced Module. I had taught in this institution, in the same subject area, for many years, but this groundwork research certainly gave me a much more immediate understanding of the needs of students. It brought me face to face with their anxieties and insecurities, and showed me the importance of recognizing the huge weight of emotional factors at play when students begin a new course of study.

Unless you are very lucky, you will not be able to do this kind of groundwork research across your institution, but you can still get a general idea of the demographic characteristics of your student, by consulting the department in your institution that is responsible for gathering statistics on the students you recruit. They will probably also be able to give you comparison statistics that will enable you to compare the profiles of your students with the national picture in your sector. This statistical picture is of course only a starting point from which to try to get to know the students face to face.

In terms of the student profile in our department of Human Sciences over the years in which the Enhanced Module was delivered, there was a strong bias in gender terms, with 73% of the students being female and 27% male. This often makes it hard to avoid gender domination in small groups, but it seems to be an imbalance that the students are accustomed to if they have previously studied in this area. Some of our most successful seminar groups in these four cycles consisted of three or four males in an otherwise female group. However, there was such variation in other factors – for example, age and ethnic group – that this gender imbalance never appeared to be an issue. Only 55% of students in the department were under 21, the rest being mature students of various ages – again, a rich and valuable variation in terms of life experience. But perhaps the most valuable variation came from the range of cultures, as Table 1.1, showing the breakdown of ethnic group in the department, makes clear.

Table 1.2 shows the diversity of qualifications held by students in this department over the years of this project, and demonstrates the considerable variety of educational background brought into higher education within one cohort. This table includes students who were in the department to follow postgraduate study.

It is worth pointing out that the cultural, social, economic and educational diversity lying behind these figures is of particular advantage in the teaching of the social and human sciences because of their subject matter. It is immensely enriching to have a range of experiences, sensibilities, conditioning and belief brought to bear on the subject matter of topics like societal norms, social and economic diversity, justice, punishment, political power, responsibility and rights.

However, precisely because of that range of experience, it is important to operate with cultural, age-related and gender sensitivity, so that all participants feel able to speak up and know that their contribution will be respected. Equally, there will be some topics about which some students do not wish to speak, particularly in mixed groups, and this too must be respected. When assigning roles within small groups, it is sensitive and courteous to ask if particular people would mind performing particular roles, rather than just assign them and assume that this is acceptable. Finally, it is

Table 1.1 Students in human sciences: ethnic profile 2003–2006

Ethnic group	Students (%)
White – British	69
White – other	5
Black – African/Caribbean	7
Asian – Bangladeshi/Indian	6
Asian – Pakistani	7
Chinese	0
Mixed background	5
Unknown	1

Source: BNU (2008)

Table 1.2 Students in human sciences: highest qualifications on entry 2003–2006

Highest qualifications on entry	Students (%)*
Tariff points less than 100	16
Tariff points 100–199	24
Tariff points 200–299	21
Tariff points 300–399	3
Tariff points more than 400	1
Access/mature/no formal quals	9
Other below HE	11
PG/professional quals	1
HE degree	5
Cert/Dip HE/HE credits	2
Other HE	6
Overseas qualification	3

* Numbers rounded

Source: BNU (2008)

important to remain approachable so that students can speak up about perceived problems, and of course to have appropriate support in place for all conceivable circumstances.

We tend as lecturers to be very keen to get into the content of our teaching as soon as possible, because we have a subliminal sense of responsibility about the 'knowledge' we possess, and about achieving a transfer of this 'knowledge' into the minds of our students. But if we are brought into a closer relationship with our students' anxieties and needs for support, we can readily recognize that the actual content can wait until we have made sure that our students are comfortable with us and with each other. Building on these relationships, learning can begin – not learning as the mechanical transfer of 'knowledge', but the *active* learning of people who are experiencing new and exciting material, making sense of it in their own way, and organizing its application in different contexts.

So it is very definitely not a waste of time to devote the first seminar session to finding out who your students are, and what they think they need in order to succeed. Indeed it is essential. In Chapter 7, when I discuss the planning of the seminars for the Enhanced Module, I will describe some ways in which you might do this. You will find that the first few sessions are invaluable in building up trust between members of the group, and between you and them, and it will help you to pitch your teaching at the level that is appropriate for their needs.

I will now give you an example of an incident when a lecturer failed to ask either of these questions. As a result, she made an illegitimate assumption about what her students knew, and she let them down. She was new to teaching and delivering an interactive sociology session to some further education students who hoped to go on into higher education. To emphasize a particular point, she spoke of dramatic contrasts between the late medieval period and the Victorian era. A student asked when these periods were, and she then pinpointed the times more specifically as the late fourteenth century and the nineteenth century. The same student tentatively asked whether the nineteenth century came before or after the fourteenth century. There was a brief silence while the whole session flashed before the lecturer's eyes and she realized how inappropriately she had pitched it, before she pulled herself together and quickly drew an explanatory timeline on the board. That lecturer was me, and that student taught me how important it is to ask the fundamental questions at the outset, to find out who my students are, and ascertain what they need in order to succeed.

One way to find out what students need in order to succeed is to ask them. I was fortunate enough, before the Enhanced Module could be designed and delivered, to be given the resources by my institution to carry out some groundwork research, in which I did just that. I was able to gain, from new students some few weeks into their first year, an understanding of their learning experiences so far, and how they thought these could be improved. I conducted 15 focus groups with first-year students from 27 different programmes of study, in five faculties on three campuses, eight weeks after they had joined the institution. Using a semi-structured approach, they were invited to talk freely about their experiences so far, their anxieties and their expectations.

The average group size was 15 students, and the students in each group already had some familiarity with each other because the groups were either personal tutor groups or seminar groups on a core module. The focus groups were structured around issues of expectations about higher education, learning experiences so far, workloads and what students would like in order to help them succeed on their chosen course.

The timing of the focus groups is significant. They began after the eighth week of the first semester, and continued into the second semester. It is reasonable to speculate that the initial shine of entering higher education and having highly enjoyable social experiences had worn off, and their attention had turned to their learning experiences, particularly if assessments were looming. While it is true that my focus groups mentioned friendships made and good social experiences, several weeks into their course they were a lot more concerned to talk about those aspects of their experience that related to their learning.

As moderator, my task was to draw out information from the members of the group on a range of themes presented for discussion in a consistent chronology with each group. The dynamic in each group varied considerably. For instance, the same grievance might be treated in one group quite light-heartedly with lots of spontaneous jokes, whereas in another group it might be treated as a source of resentment or distress. This is inevitable in group situations where individual responses stimulate discussion among the group, often because of comments made in a particular way by a dominant member.

Focus groups are a well-established way for social scientists to gather qualitative data in a variety of settings, where a one-shot collection is considered useful (Berg 2008). In this case they were conducted in an informal interview style designed for small groups, and the goal was to discover through semi-structured discussions the conscious and semi-conscious attitudes and feelings of students who had recently arrived and were still in the process of settling in.

However, the informal focus group discussion can suffer from a particular methodological weakness, when compared with an individual interview, particularly in this particular institutional setting. When groups are going through a testing transition, they are vocal about the things that are troubling them. Sometimes this dynamic is self-reinforcing, and they have correspondingly less to say about the things that are satisfactory. In part this is due to the free-floating anxiety that tends to accompany us all through new experiences. Additionally, as any seminar tutor with years of experience will confirm, students find it pleasing in times of transition to have someone who will listen uncritically to their criticisms, moans and complaints.

I tried to remain conscious of this aspect of these group discussions, and to dampen down the natural tendency for group members to cap someone's complaint with an even more forceful example of their own. Judicious use of phrases such as 'But has anyone a more positive experience?' or 'Does anyone have a different view?' or 'OK – I see your complaint – but did anything good come out of it?' did help to redress the balance, and to bring out the counter-balanced view in other members of the group. Human beings do after all love to disagree with one another, especially in a safe setting, when they are given permission to do so. In this case, students were assured of absolute anonymity, and few of them knew me because they were so new in the institution and on the whole they were not from my faculty.

During any transition, feelings and attitudes tend to be in flux. This is particularly true of both young and mature people as they embark on higher education. An opinion held passionately one day might, in terms of personal significance, melt away the next. So these were 'one-shot snapshots' taken during a period of transition. In acting on the focus groups, therefore, I confined myself to reporting on views, attitudes and feelings that were reasonably robust in that they fulfilled at least two of the following criteria:

- they were expressed forcibly by several members of the group
- they were discussed at length, in a reflective but not necessarily forcible way, by several members of the group, who may have held contrary views
- they were mentioned in one part of the discussion, and surfaced again, sometimes repeatedly, in less direct ways
- they surfaced in several focus groups.

The focus groups began with me leading students in to a discussion about their expectations of the learning experience, in relation to their previous experience. It was widely agreed in all the groups that, through one source or another, students had been warned to expect a high level of independent learning, and they used the phrase repeatedly. Sixth form and college tutors had delivered the message about independent learning in higher education very emphatically – so much so that some were highly relieved to find that they were not handed some books and completely left to their own devices as soon as they arrived.

However, in the ensuing discussions, it emerged that while students were familiar with the phrase 'independent learning', they were not so clear about what it actually meant. One of the problems with their understanding of it was that they only seemed able to focus on independent learning in relation to assessments. They seemed to have little or no idea about what independent learning might mean on a day-by-day basis, or week by week. So when I asked if they felt that independent learning expectations had been clearly spelled out at the outset of their course, many students took it as axiomatic that I meant expectations regarding assessment, as the following quotations show:

> 'Lecturers didn't cover the assignments – they just gave it out, and said they'll talk about it in seminars but then they didn't.'
>
> 'Teachers assume you know everything and give you minimal help about what they expect in assessments. I know it's higher ed but we are still very "freshy" and know very little.'

When they were steered back to expectations regarding their independence in learning in general, students were keen to stress that expectations from tutors were conveyed early on, in tutorials. But somehow there was again a mismatch between their idea of independent learning and the tutors' ideas. For instance, when they were subsequently given material to read, following a session about expectations and independence, students were taken aback by the lack of follow-up, as these comments, made in surprised and rather indignant tones, reveal:

> 'No one checks to see if you've read it.'
>
> 'They never come back to it – it's just take it or leave it!'
>
> 'I thought they'd go over what we read, and repeat things more.'

In the focus groups as a whole, anxiety about assessment was the topic that students would quite happily have talked about for the entire session if they had not been steered on to other topics. They described their depression and anxiety in graphic terms in relation to examinations and essays. It was clear that, for examinations, they considered recall and reproduction of learned material their major challenge, and yet, because of their anxiety, it was precisely the faculty of recall they feared would desert them in examinations. For essays, they spoke of having to write about things that they did not understand, and of their obsession with finding the right source material to cull for quotations and facts. Assessed presentations in front of a large seminar group also provoked anxiety, producing symptoms ranging from mild physical discomfort to full-blown anxiety attacks.

Another issue that produced strong feelings in focus group discussions was that of attendance. The topic aroused surprising levels of anger, with those who regularly attended feeling angry with those who did not, and there were even suggestions that students should be 'punished' for non-attendance, while others, more calmly, said that students should be positively encouraged to attend more consistently. They felt that seminars were often poor learning experiences because of a general lack of expectation of attendance on the part of staff, and the resultant shortage of numbers.

Most of their anger was directed at the institution for not doing more to promote full attendance, and once they had got over their anger, they were puzzled that attendance seemed so optional – 'Don't they care whether we come or not?' – and felt let down when their seminar groups dwindled from 18 to around 9 by the fourth week, and no one seemed to take any action. Many of them had just come from an educational system in school or college where attendance was monitored closely, and where pastoral support was overt. They pointed out that it was not surprising, when this support was suddenly withdrawn, if they took to lying in bed until noon, rather than attend a learning event where no one seems to care deeply about their presence.

During the focus group discussions, students were asked to produce a snapshot of their motivation and satisfaction levels, and rate them on a scale of 1 to 5. Although many students found this impossible, because they said their motivation was on a rollercoaster, the majority admitted that they were really worried about their lack of motivation. A consistent comment was that they found it hard to get out of bed. Typical patterns in the groups were for motivation to slip a bit if it had been high initially, but if it had not been high to start with, then half the group would rate their motivation as higher than when they had first arrived, and half lower. Sometimes they felt this was because they had not been challenged enough, and everything was 'a little bit too laid back'. One student commented regretfully 'There's no one breathing down my neck.'

These feelings relate back to the theme of independent learning, and the difficulty students have in adapting to a system where they do not have teachers constantly chasing them about deadlines and performance. The impression given by many students was that they were passively waiting for someone to come along and make demands on them. The concept of independent learning was not truly understood, perhaps because it has to be experienced in order to be learned. This overwhelming impression of paralysis in relation to independent learning was all the more marked because, in each group, there tended to be one student, or maybe two, who would stand out as highly independent. Such students would make robust remarks such as 'Well it's up to you to get on with it yourself', but the rest of the group would shift uncomfortably and fail to endorse this attitude.

When it came to discussion of the workload, opinions varied widely. It was quickly apparent that when asked about the workload, for almost all students, this word was yet another term that was synonymous with assessment. They seemed to have almost no conception of independent study that was done either for its own sake, to provide general background, or to enrich particular understanding of a topic. Many students found the workload much less than they had expected, simply because they had not yet experienced any assessment, and, without assessment, their workload appeared to them to be zero.

If an assignment was set early on, students got a sense of purpose, and this emerged very energetically in focus groups. This was particularly the case if they had experienced an assignment, had it marked and returned to them, with feedback, within a short time. On one particular Business programme 21 students were pleased to have been set an assignment in the first week, as it 'gets you ready, lets you know there is stuff to be done'. They found the workload a lot at first, but agreed that it was manageable, and 'it keeps you busy'. Students on a Health programme reported staying up until two or three in the morning to finish assignments, but commented that this offered them useful lessons in time management, and in future they would learn to prioritize their work better.

On the whole, students expressed themselves as much more satisfied with the workload if all the following conditions applied:

- the workload had already made demands on them (in terms of assessment)
- they had already survived those demands
- they had some idea of how they had performed (from feedback).

If no demands had been made of them at all, in terms of assessment, they seemed to experience a kind of vacuum, and that vacuum seemed to fill up with a sense of disappointment, anticlimax and anxiety about what assessments would be like when they eventually came.

However, much discontent was expressed over what was perceived as a lack of coordination between module tutors in setting deadlines for assignments. When four assignments were due to be handed in on the same Friday, students pronounced this as 'bad planning'. In other groups, however, students balanced this complaint by voicing their awareness of the inevitability of this, because semesters were so very short.

In some Leisure and Tourism programmes, students spoke very highly of the value of outside trips in the first semester, particularly because they had been related to the module content. Quite apart from the opportunities for social bonding that came through a shared experience, they found it made their subject come alive, and helped with their motivation. In other faculties, where there were no such organized outings, students spontaneously commented that they would like more trips or outside visits that related to their learning.

There was much animated discussion over the issues of group work and assignments based on teamwork. Students liked small-group work, because it helped them get to know each other, and they saw the heuristic value of team tasks. But they found it intimidating to present their small-group work to the wider group, and students were almost unanimous in saying that the first semester was far too early for *assessed* group work with people they did not know. They said that they wanted to do their own assignments, and get the measure of their own capacities, at the outset, and the time for group assignments was later on. Others felt frankly inhibited by the prospect of showing themselves up in a group of relative strangers. Some students on a Technology programme related that if it was announced that assessed group presentations would happen the following week, some of the group inevitably did not turn up.

On the whole, it seemed that preparation work for a group task was more likely to collapse when students had not had time to build relationships with each other. Students suggested that a better strategy would be to divide people into groups on the day and give them 15 minutes to prepare a presentation, but they were still adamant that it was far too early to present to the entire class, which could be as many as 28 students.

Good practice clearly had an effect on anxiety levels and a sense of integration. The most significant finding was that the happiest students across all groups were those who had already experienced a small assignment plus feedback in the first three weeks of the first semester. This had allayed their natural anxieties about this new experience, and enabled them mentally to 'position' themselves in relation to the start of their higher education experience and form an opinion as to their capacity to succeed. In turn, this had fed into their motivation.

Conclusion

Increasing diversity in the student population means an increasing range of individual circumstances, perceptions and aptitudes. There is no such thing – if indeed there ever was – as the typical student. It is not just the intensity and complexity of the student transition into higher education that we need to address, but the *range of types of adaptation and transition*, and only awareness of these will enable us to continue developing and delivering the appropriate range of support strategies.

This diversity makes it all the more striking when common themes emerge across different faculties with widely differing areas of study. The themes that surfaced most forcibly and consistently across all groups were:

- anxiety about assessment
- equating most learning issues with assessment
- desire for individual feedback, as soon as possible
- ambivalence about attendance
- anxiety about absent or fluctuating motivation
- longing for personalized support.

I carried out these focus groups at the same time as undertaking a parallel project looking at the reasons for student withdrawal, so at the same time as the focus groups were being conducted, interviews with students who had withdrawn were under way. Although that research is reported elsewhere, it did form a backdrop to the design and delivery of the Enhanced Module, in that the 87 withdrawn students who were interviewed indicated that they had not felt socially and academically integrated into their chosen course. This gave added impetus to my determination to deliver an enhanced module that would engage students, maximize attendance, stimulate participation, promote enjoyment, and result in increased confidence and achievement. If these goals could be achieved, the enhanced module would not only deliver a quality learning experience but it could also serve as a valuable tool in a wider retention strategy.

While the focus groups were being conducted, I also conducted an Attendance Enquiry. You will find the results of the Attendance Enquiry discussed in Chapter 3, along with an explanation of how these influenced the design of an active attendance support policy.

In designing the Enhanced Module, in response to the findings of the focus groups, it was vital to build in, from the start, a methodology for evaluating it before, during and after, in order to lay the foundation for that process of continuous enhancement that I have already referred to. You will find that, at particular points in the book, I refer to aspects of this methodology, which consisted of the following tools:

- the pre-module questionnaire (see Appendix 7)
- the halfway enquiry into best/worst aspects (see Appendix 8)
- the post-module questionnaire (see Appendix 9)
- the post-module focus group by lecturers or independent researchers
- registers recording attendance and reasons for absence
- overall grades
- self-reflection by tutors
- dialogue between tutors
- dialogue with students.

As the reader will remember, the preliminary focus groups had been conducted with students from five different faculties, whereas the tools in the list above were used with our four successive cohorts of social science students. It was noticeable that many of the issues that cropped up during these forms of enquiry matched the issues that had surfaced consistently in the focus groups. It is reasonable to suppose, then, that the fundamental principles adopted so successfully for our social science students in this enhanced module could be just as effective with students in other disciplines.

2

Design principles

Introduction

The themes of support, attendance, assessment and feedback generated by the cross-faculty focus groups produced the following questions as I began the process of designing the Enhanced Module:

- Can student anxiety about assessment, and attitudes towards attendance, be positively changed, by experiencing a strongly supportive module, with frequent assessment, in a positive learning environment, and with an encouraging and inclusive attendance policy?
- Can the provision of prompt and frequent feedback stimulate students to achieve specific learning outcomes, enjoy their studies and reflect on their own learning in constructive ways?
- Can outside trips be integrated into the curriculum and assessment strategy in a way that contributes to a positive learning environment?

Principles of the Enhanced Module

To answer these questions, some fundamental principles were drawn up, as a statement of intent and good practice. Some of them may seem unnecessary or obvious: it could be argued that some of these principles should somehow be implicit in any module, especially at the first level. However, I would argue that in a mass higher education system, undergoing worsening staff/student ratios and an ever-widening spectrum of student ability, preparedness and motivation, there has inevitably been slippage from basic principles, and there is a need to constantly re-evaluate our practice and re-draw the lines of engagement with new entrants to higher education. Our fundamental principles are listed below.

1 The Enhanced Module is a strongly supportive first-level module, delivered in a positive learning environment by a lecturer or lecturers who are friendly and explicitly nurturing, supportive and informal.
2 There is a strong focus on understanding and on transferable skills.
3 Expectations of students are initially made explicit in relation to full attendance, active participation and observation of deadlines.
4 Expectations are constantly signposted throughout the module.
5 Content and assessment are closely interrelated.
6 Assessment is frequent, well supported and begins in the first three weeks.
7 Feedback is prompt, within one week of submission, and in time for it to be acted on for the next assessment.
8 Attendance support is encouraging and inclusive: high attendance is rewarded by a proportion of the marks.
9 Trips to outside institutions relate both to the curriculum and to particular assessment tasks.
10 Students are encouraged to reflect upon their own progress and act on the feedback they receive, and self-reflection is built in to the assessment process.

You will notice that none of these principles is overtly related to the curriculum content. In this model, the structural principles come first, or, if not first, in the same breath as ideas about content. The emphasis is on facilitating learning, and on encouraging mindsets that will prove strategic in learning. This is not to say that the content is secondary, but there is always a choice about what specific content to put into a module: on any particular topic there will be a range of literature, evidence and case studies. In this particular story of how a module was designed and delivered with learning quality at the heart of it, our choices over content were shaped by our wish to have material that would best fit with our aims of facilitating and encouraging a quality learning experience.

Our preliminary vehicle for indicating to students the curriculum content and the teaching and learning strategy was the Module Programme. This was given out to students at our first meeting with them. It contained the following:

- contact details for tutors
- a short overview of what the module was about
- a short statement of our teaching and learning strategy
- details about module delivery, assessments and hand-in dates
- details of essential reading
- programme of lectures and seminars, with relevant reading or handouts identified.

So that readers can place the activities described in this book in some sort of background and context, it may be helpful to have a brief sketch of what the module is about. Called 'Power and Punishment', this first-level module enquires into the nature, justification and administration of punishment, and into the historical development of prison as the predominant form of punishment in industrialized societies. The issue of the exercise of power within the institution of punishment is then confronted, and students are led to consider the workings of government that lie behind this exercise of power. Punishment is therefore a valuable topic in its own right as well as a vehicle for equipping students with vital foundational knowledge about the exercise of power in the UK, and the workings of government and political process.

The module provides the foundation for subsequent levels on many human science programmes. The module tended to have approximately 80 students on it in each of the four cycles covered in this book, and led into a range of pathways in several degree programmes. It was a core module on a range of single honours, major/minor and joint combinations: Criminology, Criminology and Media; Criminology with Psychology; Criminology with Sociology; Media Culture and Society; Policing, Psychology and Criminology.

Conclusion

This chapter has explained how the principles of the Enhanced Module were derived from the common themes that emerged in the groundwork research. We can now move on to the actual design of the module itself, built on the bedrock of these principles, beginning with the topic of attendance support.

3

Designing attendance support

Introduction

This chapter begins with an account of the findings following an Attendance Enquiry into staff and student perceptions of attendance. From this enquiry, and particularly from those aspects of the enquiry that gathered data on student attitudes and experiences, a strong justification emerges for providing proactive attendance support, rather than merely monitoring attendance and absence. We then consider the possible pitfalls for the lecturer in pursuing the proactive option. Principles of support are derived from the research into student perceptions of attendance issues, and these are made real within the design of the module.

What the Attendance Enquiry showed

The Attendance Enquiry gathered staff and student perceptions of the problems of attendance and attendance monitoring. It consisted of the following steps.

1 Conversations were held with administrative and academic staff.
2 The topic was raised in the first-year focus groups already referred to.
3 100 stop-and-ask interviews, with questionnaires, were undertaken with students in their second and third years, on three campuses.

You may work in an institution where attendance monitoring is implemented evenly and successfully, and where students have a high level of attendance from the outset of their studies. In this case, some of what follows may not be relevant. However, even if the institutional and faculty policies in your institution are exemplary, and even if the policies are actually implemented, you will still need to encourage attendance in the specific modules you teach, if only because a student attendance record that is significantly worse than that of your colleagues will reflect badly on you!

Conversations with staff revealed widespread variation in practice. Attendance recording, attendance monitoring, and the follow-up on absent students, were not activities consistently undertaken. Some staff took registers at seminars only, some at lectures only. Some staff did not take registers at all, because their department did not require it of them, or because the logistical problems were too great (see below), or because they did not see it as necessary for their own purposes or did not deem it appropriate in the delivery of higher education to adults.

Attendance is a sensitive issue with staff. It has become increasingly difficult in the past few years for staff to take a strong line on regular attendance. This is partly because students generally have to work in order to support themselves through higher education, and they cannot always fit their jobs around their classes. If the timetable is finalized at a late stage, students will already have found themselves jobs, and it often transpires that the classes must fit around a recently acquired job that the student does not want to risk losing.

If the timetable changes for the second semester, students cannot always manage to change their work commitments without risking their jobs. This difficult 'work/study' balance, with its subtext of stress for financially pressed students, has made staff wary of being seen to be too directive on issues of regular attendance in a climate of widening participation.

There are major logistical difficulties for staff in many institutions to surmount even if they wish to monitor attendance and take a proactive stance towards it. Though not an exhaustive list, these may include the following factors.

- The timetable may not be available early enough for students to plan their work/study balance. For the first few weeks of the semester, it may not be stable. Despite not being responsible for the situation, teaching and administrative staff will have to bear the brunt of student complaints and, as lectures switch slots and seminars are moved around, staff may feel defensive about demanding regular attendance.
- At the first level, where attendance is most significant, seminar and lecture lists may not always be available at the start of the year or semester. When lists are available, they do not always represent an accurate picture of students on a particular course, because some may have signed up at the last moment, while others may have switched institutions at the last moment. On some courses, students may switch between seminar groups.
- With numbers at lectures often in excess of 100, and sometimes 200, a

manual register becomes unworkable. To pass a register around the room may seem on the face of it to meet the requirements of monitoring attendance, but in practice it is worthless because any one student present can sign for several that are absent.

- Late starters – the most vulnerable to poor attendance and early dropout – are sometimes not on lists at all, and teaching staff remain unaware that they are supposed to be in a particular group.

When it comes to following up absence, there is often no clear and consistent policy. There may be clear faculty differences regarding attendance monitoring, and pockets of difference even within faculties. The stated policy at management level in most faculties may be clearly laid down, claiming that when a student has been absent for more than two consecutive weeks, then they will be contacted. The module tutor might then contact the personal or academic tutor, to see if there are any special circumstances. The personal tutor may then ask the administrative staff to set a paperchase in motion, writing to the student with a formal enquiry.

How this is supposed to happen consistently in a context where registers are not always used is a mystery. Even when registers are used, this policy is cumbersome and prone to inconsistent implementation. My enquiries showed that letters, ranging in tone from neutral to coldly bureaucratic, were sometimes sent to absent students, but this was often haphazard. For example, one student received three uncoordinated enquiries about his attendance and finally an irate parent got involved. In my enquiries I came across some examples of a relatively friendly follow-up to absence, but as soon as there was a change in the administrative support arrangements for a particular course or department, such a system seemed likely to be an early casualty.

The reader will remember that the focus groups with the first-year students who were eight or more weeks into their first year had revealed strong feelings about attendance, and about institutional attitudes towards attendance. The strength of this feeling, coupled with the strong impression from staff that attendance was a problem issue and difficult for them to tackle, led me into further enquiry with second- and third-year students. Short interviews were conducted with 100 second- and third-year students, who were stopped at random and interviewed, using a short questionnaire, about their attendance patterns, their experience of follow-up, their attitudes to such follow-up and where they thought the follow-up, if any, should come from. The objective was to take a snapshot across second- and third-year students who could expect to have had attendance issues of one kind or another, and to have experienced institutional policy in relation to attendance issues.

It was interesting that the issue of attendance still produced, in the second and third year, animated responses. Most of the students expressed pleasure that someone was taking an interest in this problem, and voiced the desire for attendance to be tightened up, primarily in order to improve the seminar or workshop experience. Resentment was expressed about fellow students who stayed away and did not contribute to the learning experience. The majority of students favoured a follow-up from their personal or academic tutor.

The interviews showed that, in the large majority of cases, there had been erratic attendance. Some had been contacted about their absence, albeit unsystematically, but most of them had not. There was a huge consensus about the need for a response to absence: all those students who admitted to having poor attendance records, except for one individual, expressed a strong desire to be contacted, because this acted as a spur to them making more of an effort to attend. The exception was a student with very erratic attendance, but he shrugged and said that it was nobody's business except his if he chose not to attend.

- 63% admitted missing two or more consecutive weeks.
- Only 12% of these had been contacted about their absence.
- 2% of these had been contacted about their absences on some occasions but not on others.
- 99% of these students wanted to be contacted about absence.
- 33% wanted the contact to be by telephone, 33% by letter and 33% by email.

This evidence from staff and students provided justification for identifying attendance issues as significant aspects of the learning environment, and for building in a robust system of attendance encouragement and support. In particular, the strong feelings expressed by students in the pre-module research project offered legitimacy for building in a thoroughly proactive policy of attendance support to the design of the Enhanced Module.

But common sense also suggests that a proactive approach to attendance is far more appropriate than a *laissez-faire* approach. Pragmatically, even the best designed module will prove useless if students cannot be persuaded to attend it on a regular basis. In terms of our duty of care, attention to student attendance is clearly a health and safety issue. From a health and safety perspective, we ought to have a clear idea and a transparent record of who is in the room when we are in charge, and who is missing. In the case of fire or other emergencies, such information may be crucial.

Attendance is additionally an important cultural indicator of the quality of the learning environment. We, as teachers, need to take the lead in establishing a culture where students watch out for each other, notice absence and make sure nothing is seriously wrong. Students in their first year may be away from home for the first time, and it is an indictment of us if, as has happened in the past, a student stays in their room too apprehensive to attend classes, the absence goes unnoticed and s/he withdraws from the course.

So paying attention to student attendance is part of the overall package of appropriate support in an Enhanced Module that aims to deliver a positive learning environment. An attendance support policy was designed, and was to be given to students at the start of the module. It stressed our expectations of full attendance by every student for each seminar and each lecture, and specified the means of contact for students to tell us about their absences. The designated means of contact was via my mobile telephone.

Some readers will blanch in dismay at the suggestion that they part with their mobile telephone numbers in order that students may text them day or night. It is best if only one of the teaching team undertakes this duty, or confusion will arise. If you are teaching the module on your own, perhaps you can handle it yourself or enlist the help of a member of the administrative staff to help you. It might be the case that no one, including you, may be prepared to do so, and that is perfectly satisfactory. You must specify the means that is acceptable and workable for you. You may have to specify that the contact is by email only or by some method that suits you, but it needs to be a method with immediate access to you, and through which you can promptly and consistently record the message.

Quite apart from recording absence efficiently, we wanted to recognize and reward excellent attendance in a personalized way. In integrating attendance support into the design of the module, we put a system of halfway prizes and certificates of full attendance in place. The halfway prizes were to be awarded in the last session before Christmas, at roughly the halfway point. The certificates were to be awarded at the final session of the module in May. These will be discussed further in Chapter 9.

Clearly, the first task was to convey our expectations regarding attendance as directly as possible. A short statement was prepared that made our attendance support policy explicit (Appendix 1) and this was to be given to students at our first meeting with them. The usual register was abandoned in favour of one that had space to record information conveyed to us from the students regarding their attendance and absence.

There will always be some students who do not attend for one reason or another, and who prove difficult to contact, and we planned our strategy for these cases. When telephone contact failed, we had ready a set of standard letters, to be sent to both the term-time and vacation addresses. However, although these were standard letters, the tone of them was explicitly supportive, because we were keen to receive a response, and because we were mindful of not knowing what exactly was going on in our students' lives. It can be encouraging to point out that the other members of the group have missed the student, that the lecturer(s) is/are concerned and can help the student catch up if s/he gets in touch. Appendix 2 shows a copy of the initial letter that we sent to students when they had missed two consecutive weeks without contacting us. If this produced no response, a slightly more direct letter was sent, and so on. It can be useful to colour code these letters on green, amber and red paper, the colour of which is evident through a window envelope, in order to signal increasing urgency to the recipient.

Design principles of attendance support

- Attendance is integrally linked with the learning experience and modes of assessment.
- A high level of attendance is expected.
- A proactive approach to attendance and absence will be adopted.
- Support is available for everyone according to their need and regardless of circumstances.
- Attendance support is about good relationships.
- Expectations will continue to be signalled throughout module.

The whole design of the module was intended to actively encourage attendance. Assessments were spread out through the module, and we took care to discuss those that were forthcoming in every session. We would sometimes begin an interesting activity in one seminar and continue it in the next, in order to emphasize continuity of experience from one week to another. The team collaboration activity described in Chapter 7 is one example of this.

The following list summarizes how our design principles of attendance support were made real. The delivery of these will be discussed in Chapter 9.

Conclusion: design principles for attendance support made real

- Decisions were made about student contact regarding absence.
- A clearly worded Attendance Support Policy was designed, with full contact details.
- Supportive letters of enquiry about absence were prepared.
- A register was designed with space for coded annotations regarding reasons for absence.
- Attendance was built into the curriculum and assessment.

4

Designing support for learning and assessment

Introduction

This chapter provides evidence from the pre-module research about levels of student anxiety relating to assessment in general, as well as their feelings about particular modes of assessment. Taking the perspective of a student, it then contrasts a non-supported formative experience with the same experience from a perspective of support, using this example to generate some principles of support designed to tackle assessment-related anxiety, and to promote understanding and achievement. These principles are then made real in the module design.

Student anxiety about assessment

I have already recounted how the preliminary research by focus groups established that students in all faculties, who were at least eight weeks into their first year in higher education, had high levels of anxiety about assessment. This picture was always endorsed by successive cohorts of students in our faculty, when they were asked by anonymous questionnaire, immediately prior to the commencement of the Enhanced Module, how anxious they were about assessment in general. They were offered a 5-point scale for their reply, and these were the responses:

- 59% were extremely or very anxious.
- 27% were a little or moderately anxious.
- 14% were not at all anxious.

Naturally, examinations were the mode of assessment that provoked the most anxiety, and this gives us a graphic picture of how students have been almost conditioned into anxiety, rather than enjoyment, throughout most of their prior educational experiences, because, for many of them, examinations have been their most common assessment experience.

- 88% were extremely or quite anxious about examinations.
- 12% were a little anxious or not anxious at all.

Another form of assessment that had been discussed in the pre module focus groups was that of presentations, and readers will remember that students were adamant that this was not an appropriate mode in the first year.

- 69% were extremely or quite anxious about presentations.

These findings alone influenced the design of the Enhanced Module in a very direct way. We resolved to minimize anxiety by providing a full package of support for all our assessment, to make our assessment transparent, and to break assessment down into several manageable and dissimilar components. Making assessments more frequent, highly varied and well supported would, we hoped, make it more of a normal ingredient in learning. By ensuring that it was well supported, we aimed to make assessment an enjoyable formative learning experience that would foster understanding and self-confidence, rather than a set of hurdles that appeared designed to trip students up.

Supporting learning and assessment

It is rather too easy to throw assessment into a module without giving thought as to how you are going to support that assessment, and how you are going to manage to provide the feedback that is so vital with first- and second-level study. It is also the case that we often 'inherit' the modules we are to teach, and their assessment seems set in stone because it 'has always been done that way'.

It may be a bureaucratic nightmare trying to get the assessment changed, and this often acts as a drag on positive change.

For the Enhanced Module, we were determined to provide a great deal of assessment support, and it seemed sensible to see how we could resource and design that support before moving on to the assessment tasks themselves.

I want to begin this discussion of the design issues surrounding learning and assessment support with a contrast between an entirely unsupported experience and a supported one. Let us use the example of climbing a mountain: imagine that this is your assessment task, and you will pass if you reach the top and return safely. In this instance, the climb will involve some easy pasture walking, a fast-running and boulder-strewn river to cross, some steep scrambling, some slippery scree and a ridge with steep drops either side.

If your only preparation consists of your leader saying 'It's easy – all you do is put one foot in front of the other, and follow me without argument', you are going to feel somewhat under-prepared and unsupported as the climb continues and you find that putting one foot in front of the other does not quite cover the skills you require! You will probably translate these anxieties into feelings of deep inadequacy on your part, because you will have internalized the message that the task is easy and requires only the most basic of skills.

If you achieve the summit of the climb without turning back, your moment of glory on top may well be clouded by feelings of panic about the descent, as in 'I got up, but how on earth am I going to get down?' When you get down, you will undoubtedly feel relief at your survival, and a sense of achievement because you have passed the assessment. But you are not going to come out of the experience with a great deal of self-awareness. You won't really realize the specifics of what you dug out of yourself; some bits of it may have inspired such fright in you that you want to forget about them as quickly as possible. You may resolve never to let yourself be 'conned' into such a risky experience again.

Consider how much more valuable an experience this could have been – and one that gave you a template for tackling many difficult things in life. Suppose the leader had held some sessions which covered all aspects of prior *preparation* including *knowledge* about the appropriate footwear, equipment and provisions required for the climb. Suppose s/he presented the climb to you, using activities and visual aids. *Appropriate skills* were taught and practised, in relation to the different stages of the climb. Individual differences in physical stamina, mental attitudes and emotions were discussed, and everyone was provided with a full *awareness of the scope* of the challenge, of the risks and how to minimize them. Suppose you have a *chance to ask questions* within the group, or quietly to discuss your questions or concerns one to one with the leader.

During the climb, let us imagine that the leader defused your panic or feelings of inadequacy at specific stages by reminders of the appropriate knowledge and skills already mastered. S/he provided *praise, encouragement* and *constant support*, as you practised these skills in a real-life situation.

Imagine that even in the most personally difficult bits, such as crossing a deep river when you cannot swim, you felt *engaged, motivated* to finish the climb, and *supported* by constant encouragement.

After the climb is over, you receive *feedback*, and you *respond* with your own feedback to the group about how it felt – for you. You are given *feedforward* – reminders of the skills you now have that helped you to accomplish a difficult task, and that will be invaluable to you in the future in similar and in dissimilar experiences. You get a certificate of achievement that describes what you did, and internally you feel as if you have conquered the world.

Assessment without support and feedback, particularly at the first level of study, is much like climbing that mountain without any preparation or support. Supported assessment with feedback, however, is much more like the supported experience of climbing that mountain, and it can produce the same glow of achievement. Supported assessment is not only fun, but it is the most important aspect of learning in any module that is intended to increase understanding, promote self-confidence, instil good study habits, deepen learning and motivate for the future.

So, in designing our module, we had first to consider how we were going to factor in opportunities for supporting assessment and providing feedback, in order to work out how much assessment, and what type of assessments, we could manage with the time and resources available to us.

Design principles for supporting learning and assessment

- Support must be available for everyone, regardless of ability, so that everyone has the opportunity to do their personal best.
- Support must be both general and individual.
- Constructive criticism, encouragement and especially praise are intrinsic parts of support.
- Expectations must be clearly communicated, with examples.
- Because people learn in different ways, a variety of types of support must be provided.
- The relevance of all support needs to be spelled out and emphasized.

Conclusion: design principles for supporting learning and assessment made real

Building on the above principles, support was made real within the module in the following ways.

- Seminars were designed around feedback for completed assessments and feedforward for upcoming assessments (see the next chapter).
- A range of support activities was built into the seminar design – sample answers, videos with accompanying quiz sheets, small-group tasks, role plays, debates and guided silent reading with quiz sheets and/or subsequent discussion.
- Lectures provided background and context to the content of assessment tasks, and tested understanding.
- Group visits to the library were organized for library skills training.
- A progress review, with rewards, was timed for the halfway point.
- The completion of the module was marked by a celebration.
- Personal notes of encouragement for the next year were handwritten on each portfolio finally returned to students.

A significant dimension of support for learning and assessment is feedback, because it feeds forward into the next task. The next chapter shows how this vital aspect of support was designed into the module.

5

Designing opportunities for feedback

Introduction

Feedback is such an important part of the overall package of support for learning and assessment that it requires its own design principles. This chapter explains these, and how they are made real within the module design. We begin by emphasizing the emotive power of feedback that is delivered within the teacher/student relationship.

The power of feedback

When it is delivered positively and appropriately, feedback is one of the most potent tools for engaging students, retaining their motivation and encouraging them to achieve leaps in understanding and achievement. When it is delivered inappropriately, without warmth and care, and is destructive in tone, it is the most potent tool imaginable for putting students off their studies, destroying their confidence and stunting their future learning. One-to-one feedback has been one of the victims of the tendency towards ever-increasing bureaucracy and managerialism in a mass system; this tendency documents the assessment criteria, learning outcomes and all the other requirements in a somewhat mechanistic way, which encourages staff to view them instrumentally instead of as qualitative aspects that are central to their professional practice and job satisfaction. In our faculty, the quality of our written feedback was always commented on favourably by external examiners, and it was something we were proud of, but the managerialist tide of change made it increasingly difficult to maintain our high standards. The provision of feedback is not just a box to be ticked – it is an intensely direct and personal form of communication between the tutor and the student.

In the pre-module research focus groups, the discussion around feedback had been very heated. Students were resentful of assessment that only produced a grade, and clearly felt let down by previous experiences. Some had already experienced assessment in their first seven weeks, but could not find out when this work would be returned to them or how much feedback they would receive, if any. Some had had work returned to them with written feedback, but they did not understand the terminology of it and were afraid to ask. In light of these deficits, we drew up our principles, aware that this could be the most demanding aspect of enhancement for us.

Design principles for feedback

- Feedback is an integral part of the module for all students.
- Feedback must be explicitly nurturing and respectful of student diversity.
- Feedback must be transparent and meaningful for the student.
- As much feedback as possible will be built into the module structure.
- Different types of feedback should be provided.
- The tone and thrust of feedback will feed forward into the next task.

In making these principles come alive, we made feedback the central building block in seminars, around which we planned the other activities. Verbal group feedback was planned for each seminar following the submission of an assessment task. In each seminar, a third of each seminar group would receive one-to-one verbal feedback, so over a three-week period every student had some one-to-one attention. You will see how we managed this in Chapter 11. In addition, we had tutorial times on our doors and students were encouraged to bring work for a one-to-one discussion; because they had already experienced one-to-one discussion with us, and knew what it entailed, some took advantage of this.

In terms of written feedback, which was provided within a week of submission, we were very keen to specify the specific study skills involved in each task. We also wanted to encourage their learning in a direct way by personalized comments. So we designed an assignment feedback form, which had standardized items on it as well as space for personal comment and encouragement. The standardized items enabled us to mark a lot of scripts, and had the added advantage of making our use of the full range of marks absolutely transparent. Students could see exactly what their level of attainment was for each skill. The standardized items were never marked without using the space beneath, and generally the comments ran on over the page so that we could comment personally and helpfully. Not all the standardized items were under scrutiny in each task, so the grid had to be adaptable for each piece of assessment. The standardized items could either be omitted in particular assignments, or weighted so as to award more marks to some items than others. The form also acted as a top sheet that students could hand in with their work, and they could identify those items on which they most desired detailed feedback. You will find an example of this assignment feedback form in Appendix 3, and further discussion about its use when delivery of this aspect of the module is discussed in Chapter 12.

Conclusion: design principles for feedback made real

- A flexible assignment feedback form (Appendix 3) was designed and produced for individual written feedback, which would be provided within one week of submission of the assessment task.
- Seminars were planned to include verbal group feedback within one week, and to provide regular one-to-one verbal feedback sessions to every student every three weeks.
- Throughout the module, tutors regularly discussed feedback with each other, checking on tone and content.

Without a doubt, our feedback principles were the most demanding of all, in terms of our time and effort, but they were also extremely rewarding and highly appreciated by students, as we shall see in Chapter 12.

6

Designing assessment tasks

Introduction

In this chapter we come at last to the actual design of the assessment tasks themselves, having planned the important complementary aspects of support and feedback. The chapter begins by looking at some problems that have historically bedevilled assessment, and also at the difficulties that are sometimes associated with innovations in assessment. Based on our own experience, we mention some of the possible difficulties you may encounter in getting your assessment package validated and quality assured. The need to assert your scholarly judgement and control over sometimes wearisome principles of managerialism is stressed. Trying to steer a quality path through these problems and difficulties, we arrive at our design principles. The assessments themselves are described, making clear what the aims and outcomes are in relation to each. The chapter concludes by stating how the design principles were made real within the module.

Problems with assessment

Anyone who has been a student or a lecturer in higher education knows that there are a myriad of problems associated with assessment. From the evidence of the focus groups, we have already seen that students across all faculties tended to define their learning experience, their workload, their capacity for independence and their ability solely in terms of assessment. Their satisfaction levels with the whole student experience revolved around the topic of assessment, and all their anxieties seemed to be parcelled up and attached to this particular topic. This corresponds with findings repeatedly reported in National Student Satisfaction surveys, as well as in the literature on student learning and assessment (Brown and Knight 1994; Brown *et al.* 1997; Ramsden 2003).

It is not surprising that students have high levels of anxiety and preoccupation with assessment, because in higher education it is definitely an area of weakness in terms of quality. This is evidenced in very many QAA subject reviews, and can be summed up in Knight's (2002) succinct phrase describing assessment as 'the Achilles heel of quality'.

This is not the place to rehearse all the weaknesses that have historically been embedded in higher education assessment practice but, as Rust (2002) points out, there is a valuable body of research literature that should inform the design and practice of assessment strategies. You will find some of this in the References and Bibliography sections at the end of this book.

As if it were not enough to have intrinsic problems with the very nature of assessment, there are also problems that have arisen, and continue to mount, from increased bureaucracy in the management of higher education delivery. Such practices do not enhance quality and, on occasion, they act as a hindrance to it. For example, in some institutions, the submission and marking of each piece of assessment involves a lengthy process revolving around cumbersome administrative systems, and tutors lose control of the process of handing in work, recording the marks and returning the work to the students. This may arguably be acceptable in relation to examinations or to the extended essay, but it will not do for a mode of assessment where there are several pieces of work spaced over the life of the module and a commitment to providing rapid feedback. Consider a quite 'normal' timeline of events – normal, that is, from the procedural and bureaucratic perspective.

First, the work must be handed in by students to an administrator's office by a particular deadline, and its receipt must be officially recorded. From there, it is passed out to the tutor(s) for marking, returned to the administrator's office, perhaps sent out to another tutor for second marking, returned to the administrator's office and then dispatched to the external examiners. After that, the process of agreeing marks and then entering them on the electronic system begins. Weeks or even months later, the work may be returned to the students, by which time they have either forgotten that they ever did it, or lost interest in how they did it. This cumbersome process takes time and does not epitomize good practice. It would certainly jeopardize our goal of providing feedback within one week of the student handing in the work. As you will see, we skated around the procedures but still worked hard to maintain quality assurance.

Another shibboleth that I advise you to think long and hard about is the principle of anonymity. There are good reasons for requiring students to submit their work under a number only, and these reasons are particularly compelling in examinations and in some elements of the first, second and third stages of study.

But the principle of anonymity should not be fetishized so that it overrides good supportive teaching, learning and assessment. Although the QAA (2006a) remains committed to the principle, it is clear that what is being advocated in the relevant section of its Code of Practice is assessment practice that promotes effective learning. Sometimes, where personal support is a prime goal, it is not practicable to observe anonymity. At all levels of study, the requirement of providing enhanced personalized support and encouragement in at least one element of the programme of study may well outrank the requirement for anonymity. The need for this recognition is of course most intense at the first level of learning. Students entering this frightening new world positively need us to recognize them as individuals, to recognize their work as being owned by them, and to respect their individualized need for specific feedback, advice and encouragement. In the Enhanced Module, we sat down with a person, not a number, in order jointly and collaboratively to scrutinize and consider a particular piece of work.

By now you will be realizing that I am advocating that you build in a degree of autonomy to the design and delivery of your module. Of course, it is true that good centralized administration and bureaucracy are necessary, although flexibility may not be one of the advantages. But handing over control of many of the intrinsic processes that make up your module means that you are effectively handing over control of your professional role and practice. Remember that you are the delivery expert in your subject area, not the university registry or the administrators. They have their own area of expertise, just as you have yours. Supporting attendance and assessment in the fullest way possible is part of your role, and providing feedback promptly and in an appropriate way is an essential part of good practice. Such practice will hugely benefit the student's learning experience, as well as your own professional development.

Assessment design principles

- Make sure assessment promotes understanding and skills development.
- Make assessment frequent, diverse, motivating and non-intimidating.
- Take back control of the nuts and bolts of assessment tasks, as far as possible.
- Build in internal quality controls.
- Build in a safety net for slow learning, early failure, and legitimately late or missing submissions.
- Identify what is being assessed in each task.
- Provide transparent instructions for each task.
- Support assessment in each lecture and seminar.
- Feed back and feed forward.
- Make marking transparent.

- Use the full range of marks.
- Encourage attendance by building reward for good attendance into assessment.
- Encourage self-awareness by building reflection on feedback into the assessment package.

The nature of some of these principles for the design of assessment meant that there was only one mode of assessment that would be workable, given the structural contexts and constraints in our institution, and that mode was by a portfolio of several pieces of varied assessment.

Before discussing the design of those pieces, we need to discuss the process by which we took back control of the nuts and bolts of our mode of assessment, because it is intrinsic to the success of the Enhanced Module. You will see from that discussion below how the identification of a portfolio of assessments enabled us to achieve a measure of control, while retaining quality control exercised externally by formalized mechanisms, and internally by extra mechanisms operated by us. If you do not have the same constraints in your institution, then the next couple of paragraphs will seem rather laboured and arcane, and you might like to skip over them.

First of all, it was necessary to present the module design to the faculty board that was responsible for approving, monitoring and reviewing module development and change. I won't go into this process in detail, because it differs in every institution, but the process itself acts as a recognition and validation that the module design fulfils the QAA guidelines on the enhancement of provision. The design that was presented to the faculty board included a detailed specification of the individual pieces of assessment that make up the portfolio as a whole. This process was the quality assurance we needed, so that henceforward we could safely designate on the subsequent documentation that the mode of assessment was '100% by portfolio'. In addition, and most importantly, this validation process was an opportunity to present our case for extra resources. We were given an extra time allowance of one hour per week per 20 students, in recognition of the demanding marking schedule required if we were to fulfil our feedback promises.

With the module successfully validated and the mode of assessment specified as '100% portfolio', the pieces of work within the portfolio as a whole therefore became its inner workings, to be submitted by students to the tutor in their seminar session, with the assignment feedback form (see Appendix 3) acting as the internal top sheet. The assessment tasks are then marked by the tutors, rotating the scripts so that each group is marked alternately by each tutor. As an assurance of quality and consistency, each tutor will regularly exchange a sample of scripts in order to make sure that they are marking to the same standard, and meet regularly to look at a sample of scripts together. The marks are then recorded by the lead tutor and the work is returned by the tutor, with its written feedback, to the students at the seminar session one week later. The students put this work into their portfolio folders and keep it safely.

At the end of the module, students will hand in the whole portfolio to the designated authorities; it is the overall mark on the portfolio folder that is logged in by administrators and registry. At this stage, moderation of the whole batch of portfolios can be undertaken internally and externally, on a sampling basis of 10% or 20% of them all, and the marks electronically recorded. Finally, the portfolio is returned to the students with handwritten notes on each one that look forward to the next year's study.

It may seem as if this method of assessment is very demanding. But retaining control of the process of recording marks and returning work actually makes the whole process much less taxing and more satisfying because of the assurance of quality. There is no huge marking burden at the end of the module, as there is with conventionally assessed modules. The portfolio mark is simply an average of the various pieces of work, with the attendance mark factored in. Students have already calculated their own grade from the marks they have gained along the way, and the final grades have already been celebrated at the last seminar session of the module, so they do not have to wait for the bureaucratic processes to grind through the system before knowing what their grades are likely to be.

Assessment by portfolio is deeply enriching for the lecturer in a professional sense. S/he remains in touch with the student's journey in learning in a very real way, and over the various pieces of work it is fascinating to be able to chart progress.

There were seven items of assessment over the course of the module, each with its own intrinsic connections to the teaching methods and learning activities of the overall module. In what follows, I will explain *why* each item was chosen and the intended outcome, and to do this it will sometimes be helpful to indicate the content of the task.

When designing assessment, you will probably have to comply with sets of learning outcomes. It is a pretty tall order to ensure that one or two pieces of assessment will achieve all learning outcomes. With a portfolio of assessment tasks, the whole business of meeting learning outcomes is much easier, because you can design different pieces of assessment that target specific skills and achieve particular outcomes.

We felt that, so long as we could provide extensive support, the seven pieces of assessment should be challenging. Succeeding, with support, in a range of difficult tasks is a more exhilarating experience than succeeding without support in something easy. The exception to this was the first piece of assessment, the surprise class test, and the reasons for making that accessible for a number of ability levels, and flexible so as to be sufficiently challenging even for the most able, are discussed below.

Assessments and super-skills

If you were asked to describe a good citizen, a good doctor, a good husband or a good social worker, you would probably use some abstract language. You might say a good husband would be faithful, a good doctor caring, and so on. It is doubtful if you would jump straight to a specification of the technical skills required to be in such a role. That is not because you think the skills unimportant, but you assume that in achieving a qualification for a role, the necessary technical skills have been mastered.

So, in devising the activities and assessments for your module, of course you must build in the acquisition of technical and pragmatic skills, and these will generally relate to the learning outcomes you have had to specify. This leaves a space at the top of the design for what can be termed 'super-skills'. They are somewhat abstract, and they are difficult to measure in a deeply meaningful way, but they are vitally related to employability, and to the enriched growth of the whole person; and, once experienced, they tend to be internally embedded in the learner and transferred to other learning experiences. These super-skills arise out of the following vision of quality for this particular module – a vision that it is helpful to work out for yourself before you begin the process of design.

First of all, I wanted students to engage enthusiastically with the topic, feel involved in it and gain a progressive sense of commitment. I wanted them to understand the key concepts and be able to apply them appropriately. I wanted to encourage their independence of thought, and show them that, even at this early stage in their studies, they were quite capable of independent learning. I wanted to increase their self-confidence and their propensity to speak up for themselves. I wanted them to feel competent to tackle difficult literature, not to be intimidated by it, and able to identify the most important themes in it. Finally, I wanted them to be able to benefit from feedback, reflect on their strengths and weaknesses, and transfer this knowledge to their other studies and experiences.

This produced the following list of super-skills:

- engagement
- understanding
- independence
- self-confidence
- doing evidence-based research
- responding to novelty
- commitment
- self-awareness.

No single module can achieve all the super-skills that are required in a particular area of study in further and higher education, and they cannot all be acquired at the first or second levels of study. You will yourself know the super-skills that are important in your field – often they are the things you yourself value most highly in the teaching of your particular discipline, or the qualities you would wish to see in an employee in your field.

All the following tasks were designed to facilitate and promote understand-ing. None of them is related to the memorization of 'facts' and their recall. Each has a further super-skill that was an overriding intentional force behind the particular task.

Assessment 1: surprise class test

Super-skills – engagement and understanding

Skills practice:

- reading and comprehension
- basic statistical understanding
- reasoning
- writing.

This first assessment task was a surprise class test in the third week. It was not conducted in a cold and authoritarian manner, with invigilators stalking up and down the room. The atmosphere was informal and students could ask questions throughout. The test paper restated some central theoretical prin-ciples, which had already been covered in a lecture, in a very straightforward manner. There then followed short-answer questions that tested comprehen-sion of those principles and the capacity to reason logically from evidence supplied.

There was next a short paragraph, providing some comparative evidence, including simple statistical data, on the consequences for the murder rate in countries or states that had adopted or abandoned the death sentence. Students were then asked to write freely on the popular and controversial topic of the death sentence, giving their own opinions as to its legitimacy, but they were also asked to consider and discuss the evidence. The purpose of this was to encourage self-expression and passionate engagement with the subject mat-ter at the start of their programme of study. But it also tested the capacity of students to realize that their own opinions were not necessarily evidence based – they were just based on what they felt or, sometimes, on the transmission of beliefs and opinions from their parents, their religion or their culture. So they had to reason from the evidence supplied, and weigh their own feelings against the evidence. Additionally this gave us the chance to evaluate their competence in written English, and to offer support at this early stage to those who needed it.

An important aspect of this surprise class test was that it tested understanding of some extremely important principles that had already been conveyed through different means. 'Understanding', however, is not an absolute. There are *shades* of understanding, and students in any group present a spectrum of widely varying levels of ability and logical reasoning. So, although the comprehension aspect of the test was highly accessible to all students at the most basic level of understanding, it remained possible for those with a deeper understanding to demonstrate that depth and sophistication of thought. This was particularly the case in the second part of the test, when students were given the opportunity to write freely, considering the evidence in light of their own opinions.

Assessment 2: court visit

Super-skill – independence

Skills practice:

- time management
- self-organization
- observation
- compliance with instructions
- writing
- speaking up.

This second piece of assessment was a head-on challenge to the stereotype of the passive student who needs to be spoon-fed knowledge, in that it asked students to organize for themselves a visit, during Independent Learning Week, to the public gallery of a Crown or magistrates' court, observe some cases and write up a structured observation, using headings provided. Those who opted not to go alone were put into pairs or threes, but each had to produce an individual observation. Back in the seminar – two weeks later because there were no classes in Independent Learning Week – everyone handed in their written work and pooled their experiences in a guided discussion of what they had seen.

Assessment 3: chapter summary

Super-skill – confidence

Skills practice:

- identification of key themes
- summarization
- word processing
- presentation.

The third assessment was to read and summarize to a required length a chapter from an academic historical account of a key period in the development of the criminal justice system, and produce a word-processed summary of the specified length. It assessed the ability to read and synthesize academic material within a word limit, identifying and focusing on key analytic themes rather than on detail.

Assessment 4: researching a pressure group

Super-skill – doing evidence-based research

Skills practice:

- library skills
- research skills
- planning
- referencing
- bibliography
- timed writing.

This fourth piece of assessment required students to research an interest or pressure group of their own choosing but with relevance to the module and, in seminar time, write up from notes a timed critique of the history and aims of the chosen organization. This tested research skills as well as planning and use of time.

Assessment 5: observation of visit to Houses of Parliament

Super-skill – responding to novelty and making connections

Skills practice:

- critical observation
- recall
- making connections
- engagement.

The fifth piece of assessment was another structured observation that had to be written up following an escorted group visit to the Houses of Parliament, a guided tour and spending time in the public gallery of either the Lords or the Commons to listen to a debate, or attending one of the Committee proceedings. This was designed to stimulate and provoke enjoyment and critical engagement.

Assessment 6: reflection on feedback

Super-skill – self-awareness

Skills practice:

- reasoning from evidence
- facing up to strengths and weaknesses
- self-reflection
- owning own efforts
- applying insights to other areas
- timed writing.

This sixth piece of assessment required students to write a timed reflection in seminar time on all the feedback they had received, identifying personal strengths, weaknesses and individual learning styles, and commenting on what had improved over the module.

Assessment 7: attendance and note-taking

Super-skill – commitment

Skills practice:

- consistency
- reliability
- self-organization
- time management.

The seventh piece of assessment required students to present their complete folder of lecture notes for the whole year: their folders were inspected in the penultimate seminar of the module, and graded as to organization, completeness and competence. Advice was offered, where appropriate, as to how to improve this aspect of self organization. The mark was discussed and agreed with the student, and it was combined with a mark for attendance based on the register that was taken at every lecture and seminar.

Breaking down the assessment into seven tasks meant that non-submission of one task by the required deadline could trigger another attempt for a mark that would be capped at 40% – the minimum pass mark – if the attempt was good enough to pass. If there were mitigating circumstances, the second attempt was not capped. If a particular assessment failed, the student could take advantage of feedback and submit it again. This re-submission was optional – if students wanted to take the chance that their average overall mark would be high enough to carry a fail, they could do so. In this way, students experiencing personal difficulties at points throughout the year could still be kept involved and committed to success.

The final portfolio was assembled by students in the last seminar of the year; all the pieces of work were in it and all the lecture notes collected over the year were assembled. In this way, students held in their hands the entire weight of their considerable work over the year, and were encouraged to feel pride and satisfaction in what they had done. The seventh assessment mark was worked out in this final seminar, and formed the basis for the award of specially designed certificates of achievement, which commended named students for their attendance record, their effort and their commitment. Although these awards were unrelated to the grades for the academic pieces, it transpired that all the students who gained the certificates also had very high marks for their whole portfolio of work. This last session was very much a celebration, and assessment was an integral part of the reason for celebrating.

Conclusion: design principles for assessment made real

- A portfolio mode of assessment was designed, with seven diverse elements.
- Hand-in dates were specified in the module programme.
- Assessment was intrinsically connected to all seminars and lectures.
- Assessments were prefaced by clear explanations.
- Assignment feedback forms were provided as the top sheet for assessments.
- Each assessment task targeted particular skills and one super-skill.
- The last seminar celebrated achievement of the whole portfolio of assessments.

7

Designing seminars

Introduction

This chapter begins by comparing the dreary seminars of yesteryear with today's seminars, which should be lively, interactive and flexibly structured with a range of learning activities. We then go on to consider the structure of a typical seminar, before encountering some examples of icebreakers and seminar activities. The chapter concludes by stating how the design principles for seminars would be made real within the delivery.

Seminars then and now

As an undergraduate and postgraduate, I experienced seminars in four universities, two of which were members of the elite Russell Group, one of which was a post-1960s redbrick and one a post-1992 university. In all cases, seminars revolved around the event of a student reading aloud, usually at high speed and in a monotone, the essay they had prepared earlier on the topic for that week. There was then supposed to follow a discussion of the content of the paper. It was usually pretty disastrous: sometimes the student did not show up; sometimes s/he presented something of extraordinary banality or, alternatively, of unintelligible complexity not helped by the speed at which it was read. Either way, nothing much of value could be absorbed by the other students, or, indeed, the lecturer, and about it there appeared little, if anything, to say. I used to observe that the event seemed as embarrassing for the lecturer as for us students.

When I began teaching in higher education, not much seemed to have changed and internal papers were being published with titles like 'Coping with the silent seminar'. I need say no more. Thank goodness those days are over, and the fashion and expectation now are that seminars will be lively and, above all, interactive.

Design principles for seminars

- Structure and plan seminars to be relevant and flexible.
- Include time for effective icebreakers where necessary.
- Plan a range of different activities.
- Build in time for feedback/feedforward.
- Aim for the maximum possible amount of good learning through interaction.

I found it a helpful principle in designing seminars to remember that, although the seminar is, in a sense, the students' space, if we want them to occupy that space in a confident and fruitful manner, we must do all we can to maximize their participation. This means that the seminar must be highly planned, with a coherent yet flexible structure. The following would be a typical structure for one of our two-hour seminars, although naturally the timings are a guide and not rigidly adhered to:

Icebreaker	7 minutes
Group feedback by lecturers on last assessment task	10 minutes
Activity in small groups on team collaboration project	40 minutes
Plenary session to monitor progress on project activity	5 minutes
*Halfway break	8 minutes
*Video with quiz sheet	30 minutes
Discussion of video and quiz to check understanding	15 minutes
Relevance to next assessment task discussed	15 minutes

* During both these slots, lecturers would do one-to-one feedback tutorials with individual students, on the last assessment task.

Icebreakers

It is quite fun devising your own icebreakers, but here are some that students on the Enhanced Module have liked.

The word train

The object of this game is to mix the students up in a lively way, and get them to begin working with each other at speed.

'The usual punishment handed down by the courts for serious crime is a prison sentence.' This is a sentence of 15 words, used for a group of 30. It does not make grammatical sense if you move the clauses around, so it is really acceptable only in this exact form. Devise such a sentence that is relevant to the subject matter of your module and that has the same number of words in it as in half your total seminar group. Produce two copies of it in large print and cut each copy up into its individual words. Keep each set of words in envelopes.

To begin your seminar, divide your group into two teams of equal size. Give one set of words to each team. The winning team is the one that is first to stand in a long line, with each member of the team holding up one word, so that the sentence is in the correct order.

There are two ways of running this exercise, and each is equally good fun: teams can talk to each other as they rush to get everyone in the right place, or they can be silent and do it using gestures and gentle shoving. Of course, you can design different sentences for each team, and have several smaller teams.

The name game

The object of this game is to help the group members learn each other's names. You will need to bring several oranges to the seminar. Students can do this activity in large circles or in smaller circles of seven or eight. Each circle has an orange, and it is thrown from person to person across the circle. Each time it is caught, the catcher says 'I am Jane', or whatever their first name is, and quickly lobs it on to someone else. After a minute or two, when hopefully most people remember most or some names, the game changes, and each thrower must say the name of the catcher as s/he throws the orange to them. You can vary the composition of the groups but don't spend too long on this activity as it can get extremely boisterous as the throwing speeds up.

Switch

The object of this game is to help the process of learning names. The groups stand in a circle or circles. They should imagine (and mime) that they are stuck in mud, and they can get unstuck only by saying someone's name aloud correctly, and by that person reciprocating by declaring their name back to them. When that happens, they can leave the 'mud' and swap places in the circle.

Truth and lies

The object of this game is for the group members to learn more about each other, relax and start to trust each other. It is best played in groups. One person in the group writes down three 'facts' about themselves on a sheet of paper, beside their name. Two of the things are lies and one is true. S/he then reads out the 'facts', and the other members of the group have to guess which is the true one. Then it is someone else's turn to declare three 'facts' about themselves, and so on.

Small groups in seminars

As we planned the programme of seminars, and the division of labour within each seminar, we tried to use the fullest possible range of types of activities. We were particularly keen to use small-group working, where it was appropriate, for many of our activities. Most of us have to work with seminar groups that are larger than we would like, and this can be extremely inhibiting for students. Quite apart from the other advantages, a more intimate atmosphere can be created by getting the students to work in small groups.

Small-group working can help to foster good team-working skills in our students. Team skills – such as working well with others, organizing other people and accepting the leadership of others where appropriate – are highly valued in employment. Working with others can also improve communication, self-organization, assertiveness, leadership, problem solving and reflection. It is also fun. But it is not always easy, and although at its best it is invaluable at fostering the skills of compromise and negotiation, the outcomes can sometimes be unpredictable. We encountered some of the usual difficulties associated with this kind of working, and how we dealt with these in delivery is described in Chapter 13.

Small-group working, or working in pairs, is highly adaptable to a range of activities, from planning projects to role plays. There now follow some examples of seminar activities that could be adapted to many different subject areas.

Seminar activity 1: example of a paired activity

In this activity, students had to research a definition for a key concept in pairs. We found it a useful icebreaking activity right at the start of the module. The social and human sciences work with what are termed 'essentially contestable' concepts, or concepts that can be explained using a range of theoretical perspectives. The session would begin by the tutor giving one definition of the concept in question from the literature. Students were then given some sources, and they were asked to bring a different definition to the group the following week. Of course most of them copied out the first one they could find, and did not compare different versions.

When they brought their definitions, they were asked to stick them up on the wall of the seminar room, grouped according to similarity. Students were invited to move around the room, looking at and discussing with each other all the other definitions, and eventually taking up their final position beside the one that seemed to encompass the fullest conditions for the concept. There then followed a discussion as to why one particular definition seemed the richest. In this way, students were led into an informal discussion of theoretical issues, using their own words.

Seminar activity 2: example of a team collaboration activity

In this activity, students worked in groups of six or seven, and the overall project was to design a prison that would reduce reoffending. The task extended over three weeks and required students to do some research between sessions; as well as collaborating within their teams, they were required to consult and cooperate with other groups and take into account their decision making.

Appendix 4 shows the instruction sheet that was given out to students. This type of project is infinitely adaptable to very many subject areas. Whether it is a theatre, school, hospital, therapeutic regime, business, piece of legislation, environmental project or some kind of artistic production that is being designed, the obligation is to get to grips with the nuts and bolts of 'what works'. In this case, the budget aspect was too complex for a small project, so it is confined to one small part of the overall project.

By the time this activity was undertaken, it was underpinned by a lot of support. Students had been exposed to the prominent debates about punishment and prisons, from the eighteenth century to the present day. They had seen videos about the different architectural types of prison throughout history. They had studied the philosophical justifications for punishment, and understood the difference between retribution, deterrence and rehabilitation. They knew something of the quality of prison life, both historically and contemporaneously, of the problem of reoffending, and the statistics on recidivism, particularly with the problematic age group of 18–21 year olds mentioned in the activity. They were acquainted with the research that links diet to behaviour, the data on self-harming and suicide in prison, the prevalence of drugs in prison, and the high levels of all kinds of social, economic and educational disadvantage in young male offenders.

Seminar activity 3: example of a role play

This was a seminar activity where students learned by 'doing', and it revolved around a subject that is highly topical in crime control, particularly with young offenders. Towards the end of the module, students were introduced, in terms of a response to crime, to a model other than the punishment one, and we planned an exciting role play in which they would have experience of using this non-punitive perspective in a real-life situation. A lecture focused on giving them an outline of restorative justice, an approach where the emphasis is on the acceptance of responsibility by the offender, on mediation and on reparation. Family conferencing was described, in which all parties with an interest in the offence, including the offender and the victim, sit down around a table and work towards a solution, including a plan of action involving the offender in reparation of some kind.

In the seminar, the plan was to divide the students into groups of nine, and give each group a written description of a conflict situation, with nine roles for the forthcoming round-table conference described in detail. Each group had to then discuss their particular conflict situation, work together so as to allocate the roles, and then formulate a rough structure for the conference.

After 40 minutes of preparation time, each of the groups would 'perform' the conflict-resolution conference for the whole seminar group. After the 'performances' were finished, each group would be asked to work on some constructive criticism, in relation to the principles of restorative justice, of the other groups. Then, in a plenary session, there was a discussion of this criticism. Finally, the lecturers wound up the session by restating the principles, using examples from the students' own work to illustrate important points.

Seminar activity 4: example of an individual exercise in self-awareness

This exercise involved some small-group working followed by a period of individual reflection. It would take place about halfway through the module, and it may be helpful at this point to spell out the rationale for such an activity, which relates only tangentially to the module content yet is central to the philosophy of enhancement.

Where once it was assumed that studying for a degree in higher education over a period of three or four years conferred cognitive and intellectual advantages that were so obvious they did not need to be spelled out in detail along the way, it is now recognized that self-reflection and evaluation at every stage are themselves valuable aspects of these overall advantages. Moreover, enhancing self-awareness about the acquisition of skills and knowledge does in fact give a boost to those very skills and knowledge. Why should this be? The answer is to be found in the form of a feedback loop.

Clearly my earlier example of climbing a mountain was an experience with the potential to impart a great deal of self-awareness. At its best, this self-awareness could be life changing. Even in this highly abbreviated account, it is clear that there are levels of self-awareness that can be categorized as emotional, practical and cognitive, and that these are interdependent. When we feel emotionally comfortable and confident, our practical competencies seem to work better, and our cognitive skills are improved. When we are conscious of thinking clearly and logically, we feel comfortable, confident and able, and so on. At whatever point you begin to explain the way you function when you are at the top of your game, an interdependent feedback loop will probably best describe it, encompassing emotional, practical and cognitive dimensions.

A common approach at job interviews is to ask applicants to identify their strengths and weaknesses. If students have floated through their degree, never being particularly self-aware about their progress, skills acquisition, or strengths and weaknesses, they will find it difficult to give anything other than a glib answer. So as students progress through their degree programme, it is vital that they acquire the habit of reflecting on their own personal development. It is impressive in a job interview if the candidate is able to evaluate his/her own strengths and weaknesses in a straightforward way, giving examples.

Personal development planning is now an integral part of university education. I will not go into the mechanics of this in detail, because each institution will have its own system and its own software for facilitating this. In the Enhanced Module, we ran our seminar on self-awareness at roughly the half-way point, when students had some activities and assessments under their belt. It was aimed to complement our own system of personal development planning.

The session began by putting students into small groups. Half the groups were asked to brainstorm with single words on Post-it notes what they thought was meant by the phrase 'independent learning'. The other small groups were asked to brainstorm the skills being acquired in this module. The Post-it notes were stuck on a flipchart in columns showing synonymous words grouped together. Then the small groups were asked to come up with examples of how an independent learner, as opposed to a dependent learner, would go about his/her studies.

Then, after a short break, we introduced the self-awareness quiz presented here in Appendix 5. We gave a short explanatory talk about the purposes behind it, and then students were asked to complete it, considering each question very slowly and carefully. It was stressed that this form was entirely for their own records, and no one else would ever see it. They were encouraged to write on it and annotate it in whatever way they chose, in order to make it real.

Conclusion: design principles for seminars made real

- Seminars were planned in advance, and integrated with lecture plans and assessments.
- Seminar topics were published in the module programme.
- Icebreakers were worked out in advance.
- Materials for different activities were gathered together.
- A division of labour between tutors in actual seminar events was agreed in advance.
- Feedback time within each seminar was ring-fenced.

It was a fine balance structuring seminars so that we stayed true to the design principles, while at the same time remaining flexible enough to stick with one activity, if it was promoting real engagement and active learning. We had to make sure that the time for individual feedback was protected, and sometimes this would mean taking a student away from an activity for five minutes at a time. Having two tutors in each seminar was a boon, because one tutor could keep the energy of an activity high while the other conducted the five-minute one-to-one sessions. This aspect of seminar delivery is discussed in Chapter 11, and the delivery of seminar activities in Chapter 13.

8
Designing lectures

Introduction

In this chapter, I take a critical stance towards the traditional lecture, and suggest that there are a lot more useful functions it can fulfil than the mind-numbing delivery of great slabs of content. I outline some other purposes that our lecture slot was designed to fulfil, and conclude by stating the principles by which we made real our design intentions for lectures.

Lectures then and now

From the start of our careers, it is likely that we will have been fed with all sorts of overt and covert messages alerting us to the dogma that lectures are the core of student learning. Many of us will have inherited responsibility for courses or modules that are designed around the lecture topics; lectures have tradition-ally been the primary vehicle for delivering content in higher education, assuming the principle that 'content is king', and that if enough of it is trans-mitted to the students during the course of lectures in the form of 'knowledge', then we will have done our job.

On a practical level, the one-hour lecture slot has in the past seemed set in stone: we are not usually asked, by those who construct the timetable, if we want a one-hour lecture timetabled into our week for each of the modules we teach. It is just assumed that this represents the core of our teaching. And then, of course, we are called 'lecturers', as if that was our primary activity.

Thus many of us have tended at the start of our careers to cram the content of the entire module into our lectures, broken down into dense weekly chunks. At the start of my teaching career, a colleague whom I respected told me that I should take six hours to prepare a one-hour lecture. I shudder to think that I probably tried conscientiously to follow her advice, and delivered great slabs of indigestible information, which now seems laughable.

Students have picked up on these messages, and in the past they, too, have often treated the lecture as the core of their learning, doggedly attending lectures and requesting lecture notes and handouts, even though they may skip the seminars and workshops on a regular basis and never ask what was covered in them.

In reality, far from lecture content being king, it could be garbage as far as the students are concerned, if the strategies to promote understanding are inappropriate. You could be telling them the secrets of the universe, but if they do not understand what you are saying or how to apply it you might as well be reading aloud from the telephone directory. The golden rule in terms of content is: less is more! The lecture is very definitely not an occasion where a great slab of factual and theoretical content can somehow be handed over from the 'expert' to the ignorant minds waiting to be filled. This approach is death to understanding and learning, and absolutely contrary to the approach of the Enhanced Module.

By now you will have gathered that I am very sceptical as to the value of the traditional content-filled one-hour lecture. It is often antithetical to understanding, and when it comes to revision time, and students revisit their lecture notes, they can be seriously discouraged by the unintelligible, half-finished snippets of jargon that they read. Worse still, they will *blame themselves for this failure to understand*. So not only do they have a set of notes that they cannot understand, but their confidence has been seriously dented.

This does not mean that we designed lectures out of the Enhanced Module, but it does mean that we avoided the rigid, one-hour delivery of a teacher-centred block of information. The lecture slot was used for a range of other purposes, some highly pragmatic and related to explaining the connections behind everything we were doing.

These connections may seem obvious to you, because the module is like a known journey in your head: you know exactly where it is going and how the various stages fit together. But the students do not know the journey at all, and if it is only disclosed mysteriously to them in dense slices of content, they will not gain anything like the understanding you have, and they will not reach the end with a clear idea of how all the stages fit together. The following list covers the range of alternative purposes behind the lectures we gave:

- giving an overview of the module and the support available
- explaining key concepts and definitions with a light touch
- explaining at each stage why we are doing what we are doing
- introducing new topics
- explaining how new topics relate to other topics
- to enthuse and inspire
- to give examples from our own research
- to relate key concepts to real-life examples and current issues

- to engage in mini-activities that check understanding.

You can see that a key theme in the above list is *relatedness*. Our lectures were full of signposts that signalled how topics related to each other, and why we were doing what we were doing.

In terms of individual lectures, our design principles were simple:

- state what we are going to say
- say it
- check student understanding of what we have said
- restate what we said.

So a lecture would begin, not with the jargon of learning outcomes, but with a slide containing a simple statement such as:

By the end of this lecture, you should understand more about:

- punishment generally in England in the eighteenth and nineteenth centuries
- example: the particular punishment of transportation – why it started, why it finished
- how that example relates to punishment and the exercise of power today.

The lecture would continue by expanding on these three points, with mini-activities to check understanding, before returning to the slide and getting the students to restate in brief, possibly in a paired activity, the principles of each of the three points.

Conclusion: design principles for lectures made real

- Decide the purpose of each lecture in terms of the whole module.
- Make the purpose explicit.
- Plan the content, observing the golden rule: *less is more*.
- Tie in each lecture to seminar and assessment activities.
- Ensure the language used is straightforward.
- Plan visual aids that are complementary rather than distracting.
- Plan breaks containing short activities.

Since the delivery of lectures is absolutely crucial and intrinsically related to their design, but at the same time fraught with difficulties, it is advisable to read this chapter on designing lectures in conjunction with Chapter 14, which deals with lecture delivery.

Part 2

Delivering and evaluating the Enhanced Module

In this, the second half of the book, we look at the actual delivery of the Enhanced Module, and highlight some of the more salient points, as well as a few difficulties. Where appropriate, we provide evidence of how students have evaluated particular features of the module. The first chapter in this section deals with the delivery of our attendance support policy, which, although quite demanding for us as lecturers, was highly valued by the students.

Chapters 10 and 11 deal with the ways in which we delivered our learning and assessment support, and our feedback. Discussion of the delivery of assessments, seminars and lectures then follows in the next three chapters. Chapter 15 discusses the evidence of student enjoyment gathered from the post-module questionnaires and focus groups, including students' perceptions in relation to their learning experience on the module.

Chapter 16 describes a straightforward way in which modules can be evaluated in terms of the student experience, and how the continuous enhancement culture can be maintained. Finally, Chapter 17 concludes by emphasizing the effectiveness of an integrated package of enhanced support, delivered to a diverse body of students experiencing their own personal transitions within a 'mass' higher education system.

But before we come to the actual delivery, it is appropriate to describe and discuss the first part of our simple process of evaluation, whereby we obtained a picture of student attitudes immediately before they experienced the enhanced module. A questionnaire (Appendix 7) was administered in the very first meeting with all the students in each of the four successive student cohorts, each numbering about 80 students from a range of single honours, joint honours and major/minor combinations in the disciplines of

Criminology, Sociology, Psychology and Policing. This was prior to the provision of any information about the module, such as the module programme, so that students were not aware that the module they were about to embark on was enhanced in any way. They were not even aware of the method of assessment. They were informed that the questionnaire related to their attitudes towards assessment, attendance and motivation in general, and it did not specifically relate to any particular course of study or module.

In Chapter 1, I have already discussed the declared levels of anxiety on the part of our successive cohorts of students, as disclosed in the all-faculty focus groups, so I shall not discuss these aspects of the pre-module questionnaire responses any further here, except to register that those levels of anxiety were echoed by the students who were about to take the Enhanced Module.

I should, however, like to draw attention to the disclosures made in this questionnaire regarding attendance and motivation. Readers will remember from Chapter 3 that specific research into attendance issues had revealed feelings of anger on the part of second- and third-year students from all faculties regarding *laissez-faire* attendance policies. Clearly, by their second and third years, these students had experienced attendance policies of various types, and many of them had had problematic attendance themselves. It was therefore interesting to ascertain the attitudes towards attendance of first-year students on the Enhanced Module before they had experienced any attendance policy of any kind.

Asked how important they considered attendance at lectures to be, 95% declared it to be very or extremely important, 15% thought attendance at seminars was more important than for lectures, with 85% stating that seminars had the same level of importance as lectures. It would appear, then, that our students began their studies with a responsible attitude towards attendance. In the first chapter of this part of the book, Chapter 9, the results of the post-module questionnaire will indicate the effects upon attendance of the experience of the Enhanced Module.

The pre-module questionnaire asked students to rate their motivation levels in general, as they began their degree, on a scale of 1 to 10. Motivation seemed high, with 88% declaring it to be 7 or above. This seems reasonable, because at the start of a new experience one would expect motivation to be high, but it contrasts with the all-faculty focus groups, who, eight or so weeks into their course, were troubled by their lack of motivation and their difficulties in getting out of bed for classes.

When asked an open question in the pre-module questionnaire, about what would personally increase motivation, or, if it was already high, what would maintain it, students in successive cohorts cited a range of teaching and learning issues. Typically, 40% would cite feedback and support issues, with almost half of those actually naming one-to-one tutorials as their preferred form of support.

This is interesting, because most of us as lecturers have experience of a low take-up by first-year students of tutorial time, when the conventional method of booking a tutorial is to sign up on a list of appointments on lecturers' doors. In the Enhanced Module, one-to-one tutorials were embedded into seminars and did not require students to overcome any feelings of intimidation, such as that experienced in the signing-up convention. In Chapter 11, we shall see how students rated these tutorials.

In response to the question that asked students how confident they were of graduating, 75% rated their confidence at 7 or above, on a 10-point scale. Asked what, if anything, would help to boost their confidence, or keep it high, 28% cited feedback and support issues, including one-to-one meetings, with another 10% citing the issue of getting to know their lecturers properly; 12% cited actually doing an assessment. Interestingly, 8% cited small classes, which runs counter to the trend in a mass higher education system that has seen class sizes rise considerably over the past 15 years.

It was always striking to conduct these pre-module questionnaires and elicit the same concerns over teaching and learning issues. The actual content of the programme never seemed to be an issue that concerned these students setting out on their programme of study. Nor did they habitually look inside themselves and identify personal qualities that would assist them. Only 3% ever cited personal qualities, such as determination or hard work, as things that would help to boost or maintain confidence. So it is clear that they strongly identified confidence and motivation issues with what would be *provided for them* in terms of teaching and learning strategies, rather than what they could bring to this challenging transition in their educational experience.

This finding demonstrates the profound need on the part of first-year students for strategic support and encouragement if they are to take off as independent learners, a need that surely justifies front-loading the first level with properly resourced enhancements. If students can be encouraged into a more independent mindset by enhancements in the first year, then they should subsequently place more reliance on their own internal resources and qualities than upon what can be provided by their lecturers. It seems to me, given the mass nature of modern higher education, and the increasing demands upon teaching staff, that the inculcation of such a mindset is absolutely vital, and that the increased resources needed to foster it in the first year will be amply rewarded in subsequent years. If the first year is appropriately enhanced, then comparatively fewer resources should be needed by the third year.

9

Delivering attendance support

Introduction

We begin this chapter by reminding readers of our design principles for attendance support that we made real in the module itself, and then go on to discuss how we delivered these, drawing attention to the difficulties but also to the advantages. We discuss how our proactive attendance support policy (Appendix 1) makes it easier for us to identify students who are at risk of falling by the wayside. From our experiences, we derive principles of delivery. The results of our evaluation of attendance support are presented, and the chapter concludes by stressing the integration of attendance support into all aspects of teaching and learning.

Design principles made real

- Decisions were made about student contact regarding absence.
- A clearly worded attendance support policy was designed, with full contact details.
- Supportive letters of enquiry about absence were prepared.
- A register was designed with space for coded annotations regarding reasons for absence.
- Attendance was built in to the curriculum and assessment.

It is extremely important to deliver your attendance support policy energetically right from the very first week. If you pull your punches on it, students will quickly see that the policy that impressed them with its firmness was in fact a paper policy only. They will respect you less, and their attendance will suffer accordingly. Don't be embarrassed about being proactive about attendance, and don't be put off if colleagues sneer that you are treating the students like schoolchildren. You aren't: you are just showing that you value and appreciate their presence. Which kind of party would you rather attend – the one where your host is demonstrably glad that you came, or the one where s/he turns away from you with a blank face as you come through the door?

For some students, not having to go alone to seminars and lectures is the deciding factor in the early weeks. This makes the icebreaking activities I described when discussing seminar design (Chapter 7) extremely important. We vowed that no one should leave the first meeting of our module without having got together in an informal way with someone who was a stranger at the start of that session. Because there are always students who start the course late for one reason or another, we made sure to repeat our icebreakers each week for as long as necessary. Students who join a group late may well feel extremely intimidated and very much outsiders in what they imagine is a bonded group. It is very hard for students to get integrated into a group if they have attended only spasmodically during the vital early weeks when the group was forming some cohesion.

Our register was a really valuable document, not least because it would form the basis for arriving at a mark for attendance that formed part of the seventh piece of assessment. In seminars and small-group events, we completed the register by calling out the names, or, as we came to know the students, just from observation, but this was not practicable in a session with large numbers, such as a lecture or workshop. Unless you are lucky enough to work in an institution with an electronic system for recording attendance, there really is no alternative to passing around a sheet for student signatures, which you check for authenticity and enter up later on your register. As you get to know students' names, the whole business of recording their presence becomes very much easier.

The result of a proactive attendance policy was that we learned much more about our students' lives than we would normally have done, and sometimes a great deal more than we would ideally wish. Twenty-first-century students suffer a range of modern problems – debt, conflict with paid work, childcare problems, housing difficulties, addiction, poverty and ill health. Being brought into closer contact with our students' lives was at times overwhelming, sometimes exasperating and often humbling, because of the weight of adverse circumstances through which some students managed to make their way. Students contacted us on a regular basis in order to explain why they could not attend that week, or why they had failed to attend. Mostly they chose to do this by text and, as a result, we learned a lot about the health, social and economic factors in our students' lives. We learned about their trips to doctors, dentists, housing authorities and debt advisers, as well as their hangovers and poor time management.

By Christmas of the first year-long cycle, four students had suffered bereavement. In my experience, this often results in students 'going silent', failing to attend, ignoring attempts to make contact, and subsequently dropping out or failing the year. Often we discover the reason for the silence only months after the event. In these four cases, however, because of our close professional relationships with the students, it was natural for them to share their bad news with us. We were able to organize support, offer flexible arrangements regarding deferred deadlines for assessment, and keep those students on board.

Regarding the conflict between paid work and timetabled classes, students had in the past often attempted to put us in the position of final arbiter. They would tell us that their shift pattern at the local pizza restaurant had been changed without consultation, and 'would it be all right' if they missed perhaps half of every seminar, or even every lecture. This used to put us in a difficult position because of our awareness of their poverty and the importance of their paid work. We used to resolve not to be drawn into making the decision for them: we would stress how important attendance was for all their classes in all their modules, and ask them to reflect and let us know their decision.

In the Enhanced Module, all these dilemmas vanished like magic. Perhaps it was because of the attendance support policy, or perhaps it was the mere fact of relating attendance to assessment, even if it was for such a small reward in terms of overall marks. At any rate, something clarified the issue for students, and they did not even need to put the dilemma to us.

Such was the learning support on the module that, as long as students attended and as long as they submitted their assessments in timely fashion, they would almost certainly pass, albeit some with a very low grade. Proactive attendance support was crucial, and over the four years it became progressively finer-tuned and flexible.

Attendance on this module was extremely good overall, compared with conventional modules. Just before the Christmas break, we gave out paperback books as prizes for commitment and effort. They were given to those students who had a 100% attendance record. The books were classics in which the fictional content was related to our module. After the break, we got those students to talk to the group about the novel. So we were celebrating reading as well as good attendance.

In our last seminar meeting of the module, we again celebrated excellent attendance. In each cycle, about 25% of students would achieve a 100% attendance record over the year-long module, and during the celebration in the last seminar, they would be awarded a certificate bearing the university logo and the citation 'This certificate is awarded to . . . . in recognition of a completely full attendance record on the first-level module Power and Punishment.'

Attendance is related to achievement, even if students are sometimes reluctant to recognize this. I am indebted to my colleague Penny Mitchell for the following valuable example researched in another faculty, where the mode of assessment was by unseen examination. Within a cohort of 332 students, a detailed analysis of the results of 175 'less able' students, comparing attendance levels with examination results, shows a clear pattern of failure rates falling steadily as attendance increases. The worst attendees had a failure rate of almost 39%, and the best attendees in this less able group had a failure rate of just under 13%. This failure rate of the best attendees in this 'less able' group is actually *better* than that for students in the group as a whole, and significantly better than the failure rate for the whole of the 'less able' group. The strong negative correlation between attendance and failure clearly shows that, for the less able students, the more classes they attend, the better their chances of passing the examination.

Identification of students at risk

Attendance right at the start of their college or university experience is particularly important for students: early attendance problems are the strongest predictor of dropout and early withdrawal. If students start the course late, they could be at risk of early withdrawal and you must do some icebreakers in their first session so that they quickly feel integrated. You must carry on doing these as long as new students keep joining.

In the first two cycles of the Enhanced Module, when the module was only one semester long, there were considerable numbers of students with major attendance problems and I tracked them through their first two years. Those that we managed to 'rescue' by persistent contact and cajoling were still with us at the end of the second year. Those who resisted all our attempts and attended spasmodically during their first 12 weeks either withdrew just after Christmas of their first year, or fell by the wayside at the end of their first year or in the first part of their second.

Our proactive attendance support proved specifically useful in identifying students at risk of dropping out, as an example from the very first cycle shows. In the first five weeks of the module, we noticed from the registers that eight students were having major problems with their attendance. We wrote a concerned yet friendly letter, stressing that we did not want them to fall behind, and offering extra help. One of these eight students then began to attend regularly, and went on to submit a portfolio on time without any problems. He told us that this helpful 'nudge' had saved him from disappearing and put him back on track.

The remaining seven students were subsequently offered a one-to-one meeting, in the course of which extra support and advice were offered. Two of the seven students opted to repeat the year, because their position on other modules was not recoverable. Although technically the five other students had failed to submit on time, because they did not attend on the final day when portfolios were being assembled, it transpired from looking at their work that they had actually done sufficient assessment tasks to submit a portfolio, and their non-submission was due to poor organizational skills. They really had not grasped that it was possible for them to succeed, and what had prevented them from grasping this was their failure to attend and to acquaint themselves with the details of the mode of assessment.

Further meetings were arranged with great difficulty, because of their chaotic lifestyles, and they were helped to assemble their portfolio and submit their work without any further penalty. We were able to arrange some interventions in the second year that would keep them on course.

Although it was extremely time-consuming and sometimes frustrating trying to contact these students, waiting in vain at appointed times for them to turn up, and rearranging alternative meetings, it proved valuable in terms of testing the efficacy of our culture of support and flexibility. At every meeting, we took the opportunity to emphasize to these students that they could indeed succeed, but only if they realized that steady attendance and attention to the assessment requirements were necessary ingredients of success in higher education. Our flexible approach to the submission of the portfolio was part of our determination to make assessment part of an overall package of support, rather than an opportunity to spot weaknesses and then come down on them as hard as possible.

Assessment should not be used as an opportunity to put struggling students into deficit: it can be operated flexibly at the first level, in order to deliver messages about the demands students will face in subsequent years, and to offer them extra help in making themselves ready for these challenges. At the very end of the module, we wrote a personal letter to those students whom we regarded as being at risk in the future, because they had had poor attendance records even though they had managed to pass the module. You can find the text of this letter in Appendix 6.

Delivery principles for attendance support

- Give students a short hard copy of the attendance policy at your first meeting with them.
- Deliver the attendance support policy energetically and proactively.
- Be firm yet fair about expectations.
- Emphasize frequently how attendance is built into the curriculum and into assessment.
- Record student details about absences immediately, systematically and confidentially.
- Make sure students have a means of contacting you at all times.
- Reward and celebrate good attendance.

- Follow up promptly those who are not attending, and offer support.
- Penalize poor attendance when you are sure there is no valid reason.
- Be prepared to support students through difficult times when their attendance is put at risk by adverse circumstances.

Evaluation of attendance support

In the post-module questionnaire and the end-of-module focus groups, student perceptions of the attendance support policy were strikingly positive right from the first cycles. From the anonymous questionnaires at the end of the first cycle, the following results emerged:

> 82% of students in the first two cycles reported that spreading assessments throughout the module had encouraged their attendance. For the third and fourth year-long cycles, 55% of students said that the spreading of assessments throughout the module had encouraged their attendance; 47.5% said that this feature had made no difference to their attendance pattern, and 2.5% said that it had discouraged their attendance.

> In the first two cycles, 27% of students reported missing no lectures, and 42% reported missing no seminars; 10% had had to be contacted about their non-attendance (i.e. two consecutive absences), and all reported that this enquiry was supportive.

In the focus groups for the first two cycles, the following results emerged.

- Students were wholly enthusiastic about the module and the mode of assessment, and specifically linked their attendance patterns with their high motivation, with getting regular feedback and with the continuous mode of assessment.
- Students felt their attendance patterns were better than on modules where assessment was a one-off examination or extended essay at the close of the module.
- Students stressed how much they had wanted to attend each week because the classes were stimulating, lively and interactive, and they had not wanted to miss any of the regular links made to future assessments and the generalized feedback on past assessments. As one student said, 'You really had to attend each week to know what was going on and what was expected of you.'

It is clear that, as we got better at supporting attendance over the four cycles, the success rate in the module itself improved and, by the fourth cycle, it was extremely good.

For the third and fourth cycles, every student still on the register managed to submit a final portfolio of their work, and every single one passed. This compared with an average fail rate in other first-level modules of 10%. In focus groups, students spontaneously connected the high success rate with good attendance.

In the third and fourth cycles, 22.5% reported that they had received enquiries about non-attendance and 100% of these reported that the enquiry had felt supportive. Some added remarks:

'It just showed that it was noticed: a caring experience.'

'You feel there is support available if you need it: tutors are flexible and have a concerned approachable manner.'

'The letter made me come in [to classes].'

Conclusion

Separating out the delivery of our attendance support and student perceptions in response to that policy, as this chapter has done, is useful analytically in order to emphasize the importance of a feature that is often overlooked or taken for granted in higher education. In practice it is clear that monitoring attendance, and following up absence in a supportive manner, are not discrete 'add-ons', but two strategic aspects of what is a much wider culture of support. The overall intention is to provide an effective learning environment, where the value of what happens makes students keen to attend. This value can be intrinsic, in that it is related to assessment, to success on that module and to final achievement on the course as a whole. It can also be extrinsic, valuable as an experience in its own right, with opportunities for self-actualization in the form of personal growth, emotional satisfaction, the acquisition of transferable skills and a positive approach to lifelong learning.

Bearing in mind the importance of attendance support in the overall strategic thrust of the Enhanced Module, the results of the evaluation of attendance support strongly justify the hard work that went into making it such a proactive feature. In terms of student perceptions, attendance support was clearly intrinsically related to care and support, to overall achievement and to remaining connected to the module as a whole. Indeed, taking account of student enthusiasm for this aspect, it is not too much to claim that our strong attendance support policy contributed to a virtuous circle: in persuading students to attend more consistently, the policy improved their motivation, participation and achievement, which in turn encouraged their continued attendance, not just on that module but on their course overall.

10

Delivering support for learning and assessment

Introduction

This chapter begins by restating the way in which our design principles were made real, and goes on to provide some examples of the way in which support was delivered for individual pieces of assessment. The principles of delivery are stated, and detail is provided as to how students evaluated this aspect of the Enhanced Module. The chapter concludes by emphasizing the connections between support and the quality of the learning experience.

Design principles made real

- Seminars were planned around the provision of feedback/feedforward for completed assessments and for upcoming assessments (see the next chapter for discussion of delivery of feedback).
- A range of different support activities was built in to the seminar design – sample answers, videos with accompanying quiz sheets, small-group tasks, role plays, debates and guided silent reading with quiz sheets and/or subsequent discussion.
- Lectures provided background and context to the content of assessment tasks, and tested understanding.
- Group visits to the library were planned for library skills training.

- A progress review, with rewards, was timed for the halfway point.
- The completion of the module was marked by a celebration.
- Personal notes of encouragement for the next year were handwritten on each portfolio finally returned to students.

In Chapter 7, you could see how we broke down our seminar time so as to provide assessment support, feedback and a broad range of activities.

Let us now look at some examples of assessment tasks, and detail how support for them was delivered. For the third task in the portfolio of assessment, students on the Enhanced Module were required to write a summary of 1000 words of a long and complex chapter providing useful historical background for the module as a whole. The skills we wanted students to be aware of, and improve, were those of identifying major themes and summarizing them in a structured way. Although there were other strategies that we could have used, the following list describes how we went about the process of supporting this assessment task in ways that would encourage self-awareness.

- Three lectures were delivered that provided historical context for the chapter and reviewed understanding.
- A glossary that explained difficult terms in the chapter itself was provided.
- In seminars, students in small groups looked at different passages in the chapter, and practised the production of extremely short summaries of main themes.
- We reviewed the techniques of identification of main themes and summarization in seminar time.

Sometimes we provided support for activities in seminars that were extremely important but were not assessed. An example of this is the team collaboration activity of designing aspects of a prison, which you will find described in Chapter 7 and Appendix 4. This could well have been assessed but we chose to make it an activity where students could go out on a limb and produce something really innovative without feeling they were risking their grade. In order to support this activity, we delivered the following support:

- a video on the history of the design and usage over time of one of the oldest prisons in the UK, with quiz sheet
- library visit for training in library skills
- two lectures on the nature and aims of imprisonment.

In relation to the quality of learning and assessment embodied in Assessment 6, the observation of the visit to Parliament, we learnt a lot from our experiences in the first two cycles. You will remember that, for these two cycles, the module was delivered over one semester. While the visit to the Houses of Parliament was rated very highly by students in these two cycles, it was clear to us that they needed a lot more background information from us if they were to benefit from the experience and make the kind of connections between law-making in government and the power to punish that we wished. While the visit was taking place, we observed students' baffled perplexity at many aspects of what they saw and heard. Many were clearly intimidated by the whole experience, while others were resentful at being brought face to face with political processes that they could not understand, even though they enjoyed the trip as a whole. The arcane rituals, the procedural formalities and the sometimes obscure language in the Chambers were all commented on negatively by the students in their feedback questionnaire. The assessment itself was frequently tackled in a somewhat shallow way.

Quite apart from their inability to make the necessary connections, we were dismayed at their inability to identify in any way with the political process, with public debates about law, order, terrorism and free speech, or with liberty and the rule of law. The majority of them professed to hate politics or to be totally indifferent to it. This was all the more unwelcome because these were, after all, social science students. So when the module was extended to a year long model, we resolved to build in many more activities that would help the learning process of understanding their own system of government and how they were represented.

We also managed to support the assessment task built around our visit to Parliament in a much more thorough way. We built a series of lectures around the theme of political power and its workings in Parliament, showing the connection between political power, law-making and the institution of punishment. We were able to thread through this a lot of helpful explanatory material about the ways in which Parliament works, so that the actual visit would be much more meaningful. At around this time, the debate over terrorism and appropriate law-making in relation to detention and control was at its height, and we were fortunate to be present in the public gallery of the House of Commons for a related session on this very subject.

That particular assessment, therefore, was a classic example of an experience that was so much deeper when appropriate support was provided, thanks to increased resources in the shape of a module that was doubled in length.

Delivery principles for supporting learning and assessment

- Part of each seminar was designated for discussion and guidance on the next assessment task.
- In terms of completed assessment tasks, part of each seminar was devoted to

group feedback,* encouragement and praise where appropriate. The specific skills practised were emphasized, and suggestions made as to recording these in their personal development portfolios. Sample answers to some tasks were provided, and discussed in small-group work.

- In each seminar, one-third of the group would be seen individually by a tutor for one-to-one feedback* regarding their last piece of assessment.
- Seminar activities that related to the subject matter of the forthcoming assessment task included videos with accompanying quiz sheets, small-group tasks, role plays, debates and guided silent reading with quiz sheets and/or subsequent discussion.
- Lectures provided background and context for assessment tasks.
- Group visits to the library were organized for supervised sessions on researching skills (highly relevant to Assessment task 4).
- Progress was reviewed at the halfway point, and books were awarded as prizes for achievement and effort. (See Chapter 9 for a discussion of this in relation to attendance support.)
- Specially designed certificates adorned with the institution's logo were awarded to those with a full attendance record throughout the module.
- The final seminar was a 'fun' session, with refreshments, photographs, certificates awarded and shared satisfaction in assembling the whole portfolio of work.
- Personal notes of encouragement for the next year were handwritten on each portfolio before they were finally returned to students.

Evaluation of support for learning and assessment

The strongest theme in the focus groups during the pre-module research with students across all faculties had undoubtedly been anxiety about assessment. Additionally, the pre-module questionnaire with our own social science students had established that 66% of the students were moderately, very or extremely anxious about assessment in general. If assessment support had been effective, it would be expected that anxiety about assessment in general would diminish, and this is indeed what happened. In answer to the same question on levels of anxiety about assessment in general, in the post-module questionnaire at the end of the module, the percentage of those who were moderately, very or extremely anxious had decreased to 36%.

A separate question in a different part of the questionnaire invited them to declare if, as a result of this module, they were *less* anxious or *more* anxious about assessments in general. In the first two cycles (one semester only), 89%

* Since feedback is such an important ingredient of learning support, the next chapter details how this was delivered.

declared themselves less anxious in general about assessments than at the start of the module. In the third cycle (year-long) 65% declared themselves less anxious, with 17.5% reporting more anxiety and 17.5% reporting no change. It may be that, over the longer period of a year, it is harder to answer this question definitively, when the memory of initial anxiety may have faded and new anxieties may have taken root. Additionally, over the period of a year, students are experiencing assessments in other modes on their other modules.

This package of assessment was very demanding, and we wanted to know the student responses to the considerable workload. If they had found the considerable workload intolerable, we would know that our attempts to provide enough support had not been effective. After the module had finished, focus groups were held in which the group was led towards a discussion of workload issues. Groups were unanimous that the workload was less than in a conventional module, which in our faculty might commonly be assessed by one long essay, one final exam or two shorter pieces of work. When it was pointed out that, objectively, the Enhanced Module demanded at least three times the workload, not one student would agree with this claim. They justified their perception that the workload was actually less than in conventional modules by a range of remarks, such as:

'Well, it didn't seem more work.'

'Well, it was fun so it didn't seem like work.'

'I think, because it was spread out more, it seemed like less.'

After the second cycle, an independent researcher conducted these focus groups, to make sure that the students were not just trying to please us. The results were the same and this subsequent cohort of students made very similar remarks to the first. They liked the spacing of the assessments, and apart from a few students who were still struggling with time management issues, most found the deadlines quite manageable. They loved not having the final flurry and stress of a big piece of work loaded with a high proportion of total marks.

Conclusion

Support for learning and assessment is at the heart of good-quality teaching. However exciting and innovative a programme of learning is, it will fail the test of quality if it does not provide a full package of support appropriate for a diverse student group. Failure to provide sufficient and appropriate support will run the risk of exacerbating anxiety. In the Enhanced Module, student anxiety was reduced. The students rated the workload as less than it actually was, and this is due to the fact that the workload was appropriately supported.

11

Delivering feedback

Introduction

In this chapter, we will first of all restate the principles regarding feedback that were made real in the design of the module, before explaining in detail how these principles were delivered in terms of written, group and one-to-one spoken feedback. We discuss some pitfalls to be avoided while marking large numbers of scripts, and emphasize the impact of one-to-one feedback, which should be delivered with care, empathy, honesty and clarity. We then look at the student evaluation, which grew more and more appreciative over the four years, as we refined and improved the quality and quantity of our feedback. The chapter concludes by pointing out the very real way in which our feedback to students actually feeds back into our own practice.

Design principles made real

- A flexible assignment feedback form (Appendix 3) was designed and produced for individual written feedback, which would be provided within one week of submission of the assessment.
- Seminars were planned to include verbal group feedback within one week, and to provide regular one-to-one verbal feedback sessions to every student every three weeks.
- Throughout the module tutors regularly discussed feedback with each other, checking on tone and content.

Putting feedback at the heart of the module was a response to the needs expressed by students in the pre-module research. The giving and receiving of feedback is a highly *emotional* transaction, as Higgins, Hartley and Skelton

(2002) point out, and they are right to emphasize the importance of the language used in a situation where students have made an emotional investment in a particular assignment. They argue that, in feedback, students expect some 'return' on that investment, which involves issues of emotion, identity, power, authority, subjectivity and discourse.

Most of us tend to be more sensitive to criticism than usual when we are doing something new, such as learning to drive or attempting to learn a new language, and we can empathize with the emotion that is intrinsic in receiving feedback about performance and ability.

Students are all the more prone to this emotion because they have placed themselves in a whole system that is built around the notion that they will be put to the test in challenging situations, and a judgement that is outside their control will be made as to their eventual success or failure. Curt, destructive and negative comments without any suggestions as to how to improve will produce negative emotions: students will feel demoralized; they will feel their identity is under assault; and they will be aware that, in this particular power relationship, all the authority rests with the lecturer. Despite the authority being legitimized within an institutional context that is supposed to be objective, the judgements made will in many cases be internalized and felt very personally. If there are no clues as to how the student can access the appropriate discourse involved in the learning task, or take charge of improving his/her performance in the future, s/he will feel helpless and demotivated.

So, throughout the module, we continued as teachers to discuss with each other the language of our feedback, and to pick each other up on feedback that veered towards the negative, whether it was written or spoken. This was a valuable ingredient of the rich professional development that accrued during the course of the Enhanced Module.

Written feedback

In terms of written feedback, our flexible assignment feedback form (Appendix 3) was used for all pieces of assessment. We would give it out with the instructions for a particular assignment, and students used it as the top sheet, stapling it to their work and stipulating those items for which they wanted specific feedback. Some of the standardized items could be omitted or substituted with others, and the numerical values correspondingly altered, depending on the particular assignment. The form had the advantage of being absolutely transparent, and of making it clear that the full range of marks would be used. To counteract the formality of the tick boxes, there was space underneath for personalized comments and encouragement. It was an absolute maxim that we never merely ticked the boxes without also commenting and encouraging. Our comments would begin with positive comment, before moving on to constructive criticism, and we would use the student's first name, e.g. 'This is a well-researched piece of work, Farina, and you have successfully . . . .'.

In addition, we corrected and annotated scripts, or sample pages of scripts, so the tick boxes often contained a message beside them, such as 'See your p. 5, paragraph 2, for an example.'

Written feedback is the type of feedback that is, in general terms, the most complex and most susceptible to misinterpretation on the part of the student, and to lack of care on our part as tutors. Marking a high volume of scripts with a rapidly approaching deadline, particularly when the scripts are anonymous, can turn into hard labour for us as tutors, and we can quite easily forget that, in picking up yet another script, we are picking up something individual to a student who has tried to put something of him/herself into it. The high volume causes us to forget the individuality of each script. It is all too easy for tutors to scribble succinct comments that appear to them to pinpoint weaknesses in an economic and helpful fashion, but that strike the student, nervous about the tutor's response, as terse, unduly critical, disapproving or even hostile. Written criticism, there in black and white, that can be read over and over again, although it is intended to apply to the activity under scrutiny, can easily seem to them like criticism of their very selves.

There have been unintended yet natural consequences of making higher education into a kind of commodity that is artificially modular. Discussion in the literature often ruefully acknowledges that students en masse are strategic consumers, and much of their motivation may come from their grades (Yorke 2007). Across all subject areas, it has been pointed out that a surface approach to learning is common (Gibbs 1992).

Certainly these criticisms are valuable *analytically* as we try to make sense of a mass higher education system. But they can be unhelpful images to carry in our heads as we mark individual scripts, and can so easily fuel a faintly punitive response. If we are marking the script of a student who struggled to qualify for university by scraping through an Access course, it is clearly unfair to unconsciously penalize them for not delivering the type of work produced 20 years ago by students who were coached and groomed for a university system that continued the learning modes they were so familiar with. So it is always worth reminding ourselves, when we give feedback, that we did not design these assessments as opportunities to bring students down, but as strategic opportunities for facilitating good learning (Gibbs 1999).

This does not mean that we must only be approving and full of praise in our feedback. Of course feedback must contain constructive criticism, but this must observe appropriate boundaries. It must focus on what the student was asked to do and how effectively they have done it. As well as concentrating on the assessment task itself, the provision of feedback is an opportunity to challenge negative mindsets.

Group feedback

In the week following the hand-in of an assessment task, each seminar would begin with the student scripts being handed back. Students had a few minutes to look over their individual feedback, before we delivered some group feedback and reinforcement of what had been required in the task. Group feedback to the class on a particular assignment, once that assignment has been returned with individual feedback to every individual, was a valuable opportunity for us to reiterate the common errors while students had their returned assignments in front of them.

Group feedback was also a chance to let students know that they were not alone in a particular weakness, and we could expand on comments written on feedback sheets, verbally and by the provision of written examples on the overhead. It is an interesting truism that we can often recognize errors in another's work that we cannot recognize in our own. So putting up a piece of text on the overhead, and asking the class to point out the many errors that have been typical in that particular assignment, encouraged students to develop better error-recognition strategies. Sometimes we gave out sheets of 'common errors'.

Group feedback also offered an opportunity to 'get tough' with errors that are being repeated again and again. It is possible, during group feedback, to use words like 'lazy', 'careless' and 'thoughtless' (in relation to the errors themselves, of course, rather than the writers), whereas such language in a one-to-one situation would be destructive and demeaning. 'Getting tough' on constantly reiterated errors lets the group know that these errors are shared by many, but that we are going to penalize them progressively because we have stressed them over and over again. If the group is bonded and friendly, group feedback can be an opportunity to single out students who have done a particular aspect very well, and it can be particularly valuable to single out for praise weak students who happen to have done well in one particular aspect.

Giving feedback, in language and ways that are accessible to students, was something that we got better at, as the section on evaluation, below, will show.

One-to-one spoken feedback

At some point in each seminar, one tutor would facilitate and progress an activity, while the other tutor sat in an adjacent room and had five-minute one-to-one sessions with roughly eight students. Alternatively, if an activity was student-managed, we could both see students for one-to-one spoken feedback. This was a rich opportunity to engage the student, point out strengths as well as weaknesses, and motivate them to invest more fully in their studies.

Needless to say, the tone of voice, general demeanour and a proper level of friendly informality were really important. We worked hard to ensure that the student did not in any way feel subordinate. As far as possible, we felt that the situation should feel like two colleagues sitting together to consider an interesting piece of work and how it could be improved. There is something especially valuable and collaborative about sitting on the same side of a desk or table as the student, and together seriously considering the strengths and weaknesses of a particular piece of work. It is a highly respectful thing for the tutor to do: it indicates quite clearly that s/he is taking the work really seriously.

It is particularly valuable if the purpose of the interaction is to consider a piece of work already annotated with written feedback, which the student has already had time to read and consider. The written feedback can be reiterated and expanded upon, and difficult messages can be softened and delivered in an explicitly encouraging way. If the student has dashed off the work rather carelessly, and the errors are clearly apparent to him/her, it is somewhat embarrassing as tutor and student sit looking together at these very obvious errors. In my experience, this results in the next piece of work being taken far more seriously by the student, because s/he knows that the next time s/he sits down with the tutor, it will be a more enjoyable occasion if s/he has invested more care in the task. If the student has done his/her best, but produced a very weak piece of work, the one-to-one session is an opportunity to offer specific advice on improvement strategies. This may include pointing the student in the direction of specialist help with study skills or English for academic purposes. This message could be delivered in an attentive and empathetic way not always possible to the same extent in written communication.

As well as being respectful and informal, spoken feedback in a one-to-one session must be empathetic, honest and clear. A calm and mild approach is preferable to an approach that may swamp the student with its intensity. Gentle questions such as 'So, Ahmed, are you pleased with this work?' and 'Do you think this represents your best effort, Sian?', delivered in a mild and enquiring way, will be more fruitful and productive of a frank discussion than absolutist remarks along the lines of 'You can do much better' or 'This is careless work.' The mild question in a face-to-face situation is more likely to elicit the reasons for the substandard work on that particular occasion, and then advice can be offered as to how to operate more effectively next time. Our feedback must never discount the personal impact, and we must always anticipate the effects of our responses, and be alert as to opportunities to turn around negative attitudes for the next task.

It was often the case that, early on in the module, the weakest students fought shy of their individual one-to-one sessions, trying to slide unnoticed through this part of the seminar. As the year progressed, however, they often became the keenest, sometimes asking for extra time. It was often the case that the two-hour seminar would finish and we would stay on in the seminar room, continuing to provide additional one-to-one feedback to a queue of students who waited their turn.

Delivery principles for feedback

- Deliver feedback as soon as possible.
- Deliver feedback in as many ways as possible.
- Wherever possible, use feedback as an opportunity to build self-esteem and confidence.
- Make sure that written feedback is legible.
- Use the full range of marks.
- Make individual feedback personal, honest and respectful of diversity.
- Use straightforward language and avoid blanket terms.
- Begin and end feedback by accentuating the positive.
- Discuss negative aspects in the light of possible improvements and future assignments.
- Listen to the student's perspective.

Evaluation

In the first two cycles, we had not found a systematized way of building time into seminars for one-to-one verbal feedback, and our provision was a bit erratic. There was a greatly increased rating from the students between the first and second cycles, so we were improving on an initially low base, as the following results show:

> In the first cycle, 20% rated the helpfulness of feedback at 5 (extremely helpful). By the second cycle, this had risen to 66% of students.

By the third cycle, our feedback was even more improved. By then, the module was being co-taught, with both tutors present at every lecture and seminar. This made it possible to engage in one-to-one feedback, where one tutor went through the feedback and assignment for five minutes with individual students while the other took the group through a seminar activity. This had the advantage of making absolutely certain that the student understood the written feedback provided.

Third-cycle results indicated a higher awareness of the value of feedback than in the previous two cycles. Because our provision was more systematized, we made a distinction in our questionnaire between spoken and written feedback. There was strong evidence that the combination of written and oral one-to-one feedback was perceived highly positively by students:

In the third cycle, 77.5% of students rated 'helpfulness of *spoken* feedback' at 4 or 5 (very or extremely helpful). In the third cycle, 85% of students rated 'helpfulness of *written* feedback' at 4 or 5.

The students were asked to describe in their own words how feedback had helped them personally; the results were as follows:

- 27.5% of students named particular weaknesses in study skills helped by feedback
- 35% said that feedback had identified their weaknesses for them.
- 5% said that feedback had provided encouragement and helped their confidence.

Conclusion

It was a challenge to deliver not only the range and amount of feedback that we had committed ourselves to, but also the range and amount that the students themselves requested. For us, this element of support produced a highly effective feedback loop. The enthusiastic way in which the students sought out and received feedback confirmed for us the value of this dimension of support; their responses enthused us even more and fuelled us with energy to continue enhancing this demanding aspect of the module.

12

Delivering assessment

Introduction

In this chapter, we begin by looking again at the design principles that we made real in the planning of the assessment by portfolio. We revisit the seven diverse pieces of assessment described in Chapter 6, and consider the particular pitfalls of each piece in terms of its delivery. We state our delivery principles in relation to assessment, and conclude by indicating the connections between assessment and the quality of the learning experience, which are evaluated in terms of student enjoyment in Chapter 15.

Design principles made real

- A portfolio mode of assessment was designed, with seven diverse elements.
- Hand-in dates were specified in the module programme.
- Assessment was intrinsically connected to all seminars and lectures.
- Assessments were prefaced by clear explanations.
- Assignment feedback forms were provided as the top sheet for assessments.
- Each assessment task targeted particular skills and one super-skill.
- The last seminar celebrated achievement of the whole portfolio of assessments.

In the first piece of assessment, it may be surprising for the reader that we chose one of the most feared events – a class test – when we had gone to such pains to design student-centred teaching and learning in our Enhanced Module. There were good reasons for this choice.

Unseen examinations are still one of the principal forms of assessment in higher education, and students need to develop the ability to do their best in this form of test. From the pre-module research, it was clear that it was this particular form of assessment that provoked the most anxiety, with 88% declaring extreme or moderate anxiety.

The surprise class test was very definitely not a conventional examination, but it did share some characteristics with examinations. The test paper contained formal questions, it had a time limit of one hour, and while students could ask questions of the lecturer, they were to submit only their own work without collaboration with others or consulting notes or textbooks.

However, efforts were made to make it an entirely non-threatening experience. It was not flagged up in advance, and the module programme merely referred to 'Assessment 1' as occurring in that particular week. So students did not have time to get anxious about it. We took pains to run it informally: if students wanted clarification of something, they were free to ask us. We very definitely avoided the solemn voices and serious looks that academics normally seem to adopt in test and examination events, making jokes as we gave out the papers. In short we behaved as if the event was fun, and as if we expected the students to enjoy it.

Indeed we did expect the students to enjoy it. The short-answer questions tested understanding of a number of key concepts that were not only explained in straightforward language in a paragraph on the test paper, with real-life examples, but had been covered in the previous two lectures. In the lectures themselves, we had checked for understanding, so this part of the test paper was really a way of confirming for the students that they had these concepts well and truly under their belt, and that they could apply them to real-life examples.

The second half of the paper was an opportunity to write freely on a popular and controversial topic (in this case, the death penalty) and was a deliberate attempt to tap into what we knew from experience was a topic that gave rise to passionately held opinions among criminology, psychology, sociology and social policy students. When it came to considering the simple statistical evidence we provided regarding the murder rates in those countries or states that had either abandoned or adopted the death penalty, we were really testing ourselves just as much as the students: had we conveyed understanding of these important key concepts in ways that enabled the students to apply the principles, with evidence, and reason effectively, even when this might contrast with their passionately held opinions?

This was assessment for success. By this I mean that we intended that everyone should pass, thus beginning the assessment package with a personal success – and success in a mode of assessment that had not always been comfortable in our students' prior learning.

If students missed the seminar in which the class test occurred, we sent them off to the library with the test paper the next time they showed up, and asked them to complete the paper in an hour. Again, our relaxed attitude to the test acted to demystify the assessment, and also signalled to the students that we could trust them to monitor their own time limit.

The second piece of assessment asked students to visit a Crown or magistrates' court and write a structured observation. This visit and the write-up were to take place during Independent Study Week, a week in which there were no lectures or seminars. There was always the possibility that students might be too timid or passive to organize this for themselves, so we stressed that they could visit the court close to the university, and that this could be done in pairs or threes. In all cycles, the vast majority of students chose to do the visit independently, and where they opted to do it in pairs or threes, it was usually because they were doing something particularly adventurous such as travelling up London in search of a really interesting court experience.

When students returned to the seminar two weeks after having been given the assignment, there was always a great buzz as the cases and experiences were discussed and compared. Again, this was assessment for success. If students had made the visit and written the structured observation, it was almost impossible to fail, even though the quality of the work, and subsequent grades, did of course vary enormously.

Having purposely built up the students' confidence by two assessments that were designed to promote self-esteem and confidence, the third assessment – the chapter summary – was a demanding task. I have already explained in Chapter 10 how we supported this assessment. Even so, it was extremely difficult for some students, and in each cycle some would not achieve the pass mark of 40%.

Had this been the first piece of assessment, this would have been a devastating blow for some of our students with high levels of anxiety and fragile self-esteem. However, because it followed two successes, these students had reserves of confidence and commitment, so it was possible in feedback sessions to build on those reserves and seriously consider how this particular assignment could have been stronger, and how the weaknesses could be improved in future. In some cases, students with marks below 40% chose to do the assignment again, using the feedback provided, because they were keen to keep up their average. This was not strictly necessary, because the module rules demanded that they pass the whole portfolio, not every piece of work within it. In one memorable case, a student ended up doing the third piece of assessment three times, even though she passed on her second attempt, because she was so determined to improve her performance. When students, of their own volition, opted to re-do a piece of work in this way, we were happy to reward their motivation by entering the highest grade achieved on their records.

By this point in each cycle, we felt we were hitting our stride with our assessment package. Students had successes under their belt, and some had weathered failure, learned and come back from it. The fourth assessment involved them in choosing a pressure group with relevance to the module, and over a couple of weeks researching the history, aims and achievements of this group. So although their research and retrieval skills were being tested, they could take as long as they wanted to find their way around books, journals and databases. They then brought their notes to a seminar and wrote up their accounts.

This piece of assessment was in some ways similar to an open-notes examination. It tended not to provoke anxiety because there was no emphasis on memorizing material, and because although we specified a desirable time limit for the write-up, we allowed students to stay on in the room and finish at their own pace if they wished to do so. This alleviated the pressure on those students who think more slowly and, as is common, write more slowly.

The fifth assessment involved us all getting into a coach and being conveyed to the Houses of Parliament, for a guided tour and attendance in the public gallery of either the House of Lords or the House of Commons, or one of the Committee proceedings. If, for whatever reason, students missed the coach and did not make their own way by public transport, then they had to organize an independent visit themselves. This would mean that they would miss the guided tour by a qualified official, but they could still visit the public gallery of either chamber. Following the visit, students had to hand in a structured observation.

Unfortunately, it was necessary for us to charge students for the coach, but this was a considerable improvement on the first cycle of the module, when we had to travel to London on public transport. This had proved an expensive undertaking, and we changed the arrangements as a result of feedback from the students.

The seventh assessment involved us in evaluating the whole folder of lecture notes put together by each student. The mark for this was combined with a mark for attendance. We went around the room in an informal way, sitting down to look at students' folders, and it was a good opportunity to offer advice about note-taking strategies and to arrive at a consensus with the student about what mark the folder deserved. There is an interesting gender distinction here that is probably familiar to most lecturers, in that female students on the whole put much more effort into their folders of notes, using colours to highlight key points and other presentational aids that help them to achieve a beautiful presentation. Having said that, over the four cycles, the only students who took the trouble to word-process their lecture notes, following the lecture, were male, so perhaps technology is beginning to reverse the gender trend.

The second element of this seventh assessment was an attendance mark; this was arrived at by consulting the register, on which we had recorded all attendance and all legitimate or unexplained absences.

Delivery principles for assessment

- Build confidence and self-esteem in initial assessments.
- Make instructions and feedback clear and transparent.

- Deliver assessments as opportunities for understanding and learning rather than penalty and criticism.
- Be flexible but fair to everyone about the assessment environment.
- Closely connect assessment delivery and feedback.

Evaluation and conclusion

Students had the opportunity to criticize the amount and type of assessment in the open-ended questions in the best/worst mini-questionnaire (Appendix 8), and in the post-module questionnaire (Appendix 9). They rarely did so. Sometimes one or two would single out the difficult third piece of assessment – the chapter summary – and define it as something they had disliked. No one ever singled out the surprise class test for criticism.

Given the usual attitude of students towards assessment, we were pleased to find that they accepted such a large package of assessment as a normal and unremarkable part of the whole learning experience. We were even more pleased to find that assessment was so often recognized as an appreciated and enjoyable part of their learning development; you will find this aspect of student evaluation in Chapter 15, which deals with enjoyment, self-awareness and reflection on feedback.

13

Delivering seminars

Introduction

In this chapter, we look at the design principles that were made real in the planning of our seminars, and explain how these were delivered, making clear what our aims were. We look at icebreakers and related strategies aimed at promoting student engagement. We then discuss the practicalities of working in small groups. Some of the difficulties of seminars in general and small-group working in particular are discussed. The chapter concludes by emphasizing the enjoyment engendered by lively seminars.

Design principles for seminars made real

- Seminars were planned in advance, and integrated with lecture plans and assessments.
- Seminar topics were published in the module programme.
- Icebreakers were worked out in advance.
- Materials for different activities were gathered together.
- A division of labour between tutors in actual seminar events was agreed in advance.
- Feedback time within each seminar was ring-fenced.

Delivering icebreakers

In the first week or two, especially at the first level, the seminar may well be dominated by a sense of nervous unease. For most students, a lot of emotional energy goes into feeling uncomfortable in a room filled with strangers. There is not much left over to devote to the business of learning. The sooner you can convert this emotion into something more positive, and make everyone feel comfortable with you and with each other, the quicker and more effectively the learning can begin.

Nowadays, seminar group numbers are quite large – in our case as high as 27 – so you will need to begin the sessions with a quick icebreaker for several weeks until everyone knows everyone else's name. In Chapter 7, I suggested some icebreakers that we have found useful.

You will know when icebreakers have done their job. You will observe that students come into the room chatting and laughing, and this carries on while they sit down and get themselves organized. They will make eye contact with you and with each other, and their body language will tell you that they have stopped noticing the formality of the room and its setting. They will use the opportunity to ask you questions and chat about issues in the media relevant to the module. You will become aware that some, if not all, are truly 'engaged'.

For those who are obviously not 'engaged', and who still appear comparatively isolated, both from you and from the rest of the group, this is an opportunity, while everyone is settling down and waiting for things to begin, for you to wander over and have a chat, drawing into the chat those students sitting on either side. The colleague with whom I delivered the Enhanced Module was engagingly good at this, and sometimes I would be waiting to begin the seminar with our first activity, while he was across the room exchanging confidences with two or three relatively reticent students about something utterly trivial, such as what they had all had for breakfast. Somehow, he would manage to develop this chit-chat into canvassing their views on a current case in the media with relevance to our module.

I cannot emphasize strongly enough how important this kind of empathetic connection is. We all know, from looking back at our own extensive experiences as students in the classroom, at school and college, that part of wanting to do well in a subject almost always has an element, however small, of wanting to do well for that teacher. This is not necessarily linked to liking that teacher, or wanting in any way to be like her/him. It is more like marking out that teacher as, for the purposes of one particular subject or activity, a significant other. Perhaps it comes about because, consciously or unconsciously, we perceive their commitment to their subject, we intuit their engagement and effort in our learning, and we realize how wholeheartedly they want us to succeed. They have attended to us and valued us, and this truly produces reciprocity in us: we want to reciprocate and show that we are worthy of their faith in us. Now *we* are that teacher, and this is our chance to be significant to our students' learning and development.

This chance to be a significant other is quite a humbling challenge, considering the diversity of twenty-first-century students. Because of the sheer weight of numbers, and the 'mass delivery' feel of higher education, it is more important than ever to have a stance of 'paying attention' to each and every student. Let me try to go into a little more detail of what I mean.

As academics, we tend to have developed the faculty of critical questioning to a relatively high degree. But, if we are teachers, the faculty of authentic and empathetic listening is equally as important. Unfortunately, the development of the first faculty can sometimes drive out the development of the second. The skills of questioning, investigating, testing hypotheses and conducting experiments are all highly valued in the natural and human sciences, whereas listening attentively to the telling of personal experience is not, except in qualitative research that has not always been accorded the methodological respect that it deserves. Corradi Fiumara (1990: 29) has suggested that the problem of listening is like a shadow dimension in the development of our culture. To develop this faculty, we need to adopt a respectful humility in the face of the huge diversity of cultures and life experiences of our students. Only then can we really listen to their difficulties in learning, and enhance their learning.

We certainly found that teaching together produced a deeper experience in this regard for the students. There were sometimes particular aspects of our students' welfare that either my colleague or I was instinctively reluctant to get involved with, but they were not the same aspects. Of course we could mask this instinctive reaction, and be professionally sympathetic and patient, but interestingly students began to 'suss out' which of us was the most appropriate to approach for particular issues, be it help with spelling or a sympathetic ear with regard to the mundane difficulties of transport. To listen authentically is very time-consuming, but it is a good use of time, and helps our students to develop cognitive and emotional security in this testing time of transition. Students will not truly develop into independent learners without this security.

Working in small groups

We found that small-group activities were most effective in groups of between five and seven. We mixed and matched the small groups each week, so that students did not get entrenched into one group. In an entrenched group, things may work very well for five students, but the sixth may hate the mix and long for a fresh group to work with. When casting students into groups, we made sure that the furniture got moved and rearranged, so that every member of the group was face to face with the others. No one should be half turned away from the group or out on a limb. Seating arrangements of this type can so easily produce non-engagement.

Initially we would ask the students to produce ground rules for small-group working. They would all come up with rules such as listening to each other, not interrupting, drawing out silent group members, not dominating the group, not being racist, sexist or ageist, and so on. Then the students would put these up on a flipchart. Over the course of the module, we could issue timely reminders to 'Remember your ground rules!' As the groups were working on a task, we used to circulate around the room and sit down to join each group for a few minutes. If they seemed stuck, we could get them going again with a pertinent question.

For many tasks, each group will need a facilitator, a scribe and a presenter who will share the group's work with the full seminar group in plenary sessions. The facilitator is responsible for kick-starting the discussion, keeping an eye on the ground rules, making sure the group stay on track and reminding them when a particular rule is being broken. The scribe is responsible for recording the workings of the group and providing an account that will form the basis for the presenter to share in the plenary session that follows the small-group task. It is tempting to let the groups themselves sort out these roles, but this is likely to lead to the same extravert students doing the facilitating and presenting roles each week. For strategic reasons, we would usually decide to suggest candidates for each role.

The ground rule they were most likely to find difficult was that of drawing out those members of the group who were silent and withdrawn. A very few first-year students seem, initially, temperamentally unable to blossom in small groups. They may remain utterly silent, and their body language will express withdrawal and attempted invisibility. This is very worrying, because you will realize that they are extremely averse to this kind of situation, and probably feeling very insecure and exposed. In order to avoid feeling threatened by the same situation week on week, they may fail to attend, and drop out of university.

It is useful to put oneself in the place of these students, and try to imagine the situation as they see it. They may come from a familial or cultural background where they were positively discouraged from self-expression. They may have been extremely withdrawn all the way through school, and the authorities may have colluded in this because it was welcome behaviour in comparison with other more boisterous and demanding pupils. They may never have experienced small-group working, and they may have managed, all their lives, to avoid any interactive situations that involved them in exposing themselves in groups. They may have entered further or higher education with absolutely no expectations and very little confidence, and suddenly they find that, unlike school, it is not possible to slide invisibly through the experience.

It is possible to spot these extremely isolated students quite early on. It is important to make early efforts to help them feel included, because one does not want their silence or withdrawal to become entrenched. It is hoped that the icebreakers will help to make them feel more comfortable, and that is why it is extremely important to keep up the icebreakers for the first few weeks, certainly over the period when late starters are still joining the group. When we still had worries about reticent students, we would sometimes ask the small groups to operate the 'name game' icebreaker for two or three minutes before starting on their task (see page 53).

A useful strategy that has produced good results is to cast the groups so as to have several reticent students together in a group. Rather than sit in absolute silence, we would find that they would all timidly begin to feel their way into conversation. Another strategy is to manage groups so that the 'silents' are acting as scribes. This gives them an important role, but they are not required to lead the discussion or contribute to it if they do not choose to. Nevertheless, in the course of recording the workings of the group, and reading back to the group what has been said, they will make a valuable verbal contribution, and one that can be praised and encouraged. This contribution is structured because it is a record of what has been said or done, and therefore much less threatening than the obligation to make individual impromptu contributions to a discussion.

A good strategy in small-group working is to wander around the room and sit down for a few minutes with each group as they are tackling a task. It is surprising how quickly some groups will unconsciously bond together, and yet others may remain awkward and inhibited. By sitting with groups for a few minutes, we might produce some change in the dynamic of that group by judicious intervention. We found that if we constantly put before them the conditions of possibility for them to grow into this activity, then sooner or later they did so. We felt that it was always worth persevering with this way of working, because the skill of working well in small groups is potentially transforming on a personal as well as an intellectual level, in addition to being strongly related to employability.

Nevertheless, small-group working has the potential to produce conflict. Individuals have different tolerance levels in terms of disagreements in discussions and tasks. Some small groups will burst into argument, and appear extremely abrasive with each other, and yet they never fall out, and often leave the seminar room still arguing loudly and provoking one another in a very animated fashion. In other groups, one small remark may trigger hostility and a sense of grievance. We had a ready-made model for dealing with conflict, in the form of restorative conflict resolution, but we have never had to use it.

We had lots of small-group working, but no assessed small-group work. Students in the pre-module focus groups had been quite explicit in stating that the first year was too soon to have assessed group work, when they were still building social relationships with their peers. Experience had shown us in the past that this scenario of assessed small group work had the capacity to produce much conflict, especially when a small group works on a project that is going to be assessed, and one or two members of the group fail to pull their weight. Profound resentment can arise if these members benefit from a group grade that they have not contributed to.

Clearly, the timings for the breakdown of activities within a two-hour seminar that were suggested in Chapter 7 are a guide and certainly not rigidly adhered to. If good learning was obviously taking place during an activity, then it would be encouraged and given the time it needed. Constructive discussions, where the whole group are passionately involved either directly or listening intently, should never be cut off.

We had a useful example of this in one particular cycle, when in only the second week of the module, a seminar group began to discuss different justifications for punishment in different cultures and religions. The group was very mixed culturally. The discussion became so intense, and encapsulated so many key concepts that we were currently studying, that it would have been extremely negative not to let it proceed. This was one of many occasions where the diversity of our students proved so enriching in terms of learning quality. It was also an opportunity for us to point out to students our good fortune in having such a range of attitudes and passionately held opinions present in one room, even if some found much to disagree with in others. Reflecting on this extraordinary session afterwards, we, as teachers, felt that at such an early stage in the module, students would not have been so open and trusting with each other had the icebreakers not been done so thoroughly.

Evaluation and conclusion

Seminars were frequently mentioned by students as the 'best' aspect of the module in the mini-questionnaire delivered at the halfway point (Appendix 8). Sometimes students would single out particular seminars for mention. The team collaboration activity – designing a prison – was particularly popular. In general, students put an enormous amount of effort into this particular activity, even though it was not assessed. Some asked if it could be assessed, as they felt it brought out the best in them. By the last cycle, some groups were spontaneously producing computer-aided designs that they had worked on outside the class.

Seminars also came out well in terms of enjoyment (see Chapter 15) and attracted the highest rating of any feature apart from trips. I have already mentioned how lively, interactive and well attended they were. Part of their success was surely due to the broad range of activities provided, as well as to the teaching 'double act', which also attracted high ratings from the students. This latter aspect was a great source of professional development for us as teachers, and sometimes we left a seminar feeling that we had learned at least as much as the students.

14

Delivering lectures

Introduction

In this chapter, we will revisit the design principles made real in the planning of our lectures, and consider the extremely important principles for delivery. In doing so, we will consider some of the usual hazards that might pose a particular challenge to the overall ethos of the Enhanced Module, and how we might overcome these hazards.

Design principles for lectures made real

- Decide the purpose of each lecture in terms of the whole module.
- Make the purpose explicit.
- Plan content, observing the golden rule: *less is more*.
- Tie in each lecture to seminar and assessment activities.
- Ensure the language used is straightforward.
- Plan visual aids that are complementary rather than distracting.
- Plan breaks containing short activities.

In terms of the first few design principles, you can see that I am advocating a degree of connectedness that has in the past been traditionally lacking in lectures. As a student, it sometimes seemed to me as if the lecturer knew a secret about the relevance of each lecture, but s/he was determined not to impart it, only to hint at it in the hope that we students would realize what the secret was. If it is possible to explain what you want to say in straightforward language, then do so. If it is not possible, then do not say it. Long, convoluted sentences, with lots of subordinate clauses, are useless in a lecture. You may know where they are going, but your audience will not, and you need to make the point of the lecture absolutely transparent.

Most of us feel insecure in a lecture situation, especially early in our careers. We may even experience mild panic and fear. Maybe it is something to do with facing a lot of people as a lone individual. It is natural to feel a little threatened and defensive, but this must not lead to the lecture turning into a solemn occasion. In the past, the lecture has often seemed to be a platform for pomposity, verbosity and self-importance. In my first university experience, the lecturer used to sweep in like a black bat, resplendent in gown, and, fixing his eyes on his notes before him, he would speak pompously for an hour, without ever once making eye contact with his audience. Gathering his notes together with an air of importance at the end, he would sweep out, followed by the rippling folds of his gown. I can see now that he was probably terribly shy and that this was his defence.

Perhaps some of our insecurity stems from the fact that traditional lecturing is rather an unnatural activity to those of us who instinctively cleave towards an interactive teaching style, and of course, within the context of the Enhanced Module, it has the potential to strike entirely the wrong note. So although I do not intend to revisit the advice of those many helpful books that have been written about how to lecture well, I do want to offer some remarks that have helped us in threading lectures profitably into the delivery of the Enhanced Module. The reason for going into this in a bit of detail is that it is extremely important not to compromise the module by having one element that jars with the overall principles. It is no good having open, friendly and interactive seminars if you then follow this up with a lecture characterized by frosty remoteness.

The first challenge for us was to avoid formality in a module designed to approach learning from a student perspective. Lectures can be delivered with an ease and lightness if you approach them as conversations that are very probably going to be enjoyable, and if you keep in mind that your audience is composed of those very same people that you have begun to make a warm and fruitful relationship with.

When we are nervous, it is quite natural to become rather stiff and wooden. If this is the case, then it is useful to shut your office door for a few minutes before the lecture, and do something that will counter this tendency, such as a spot of stretching, deep breathing or even yoga. Personally, I find it quite helpful to shut my office door and jump around to some rock music for a couple of minutes. This makes me feel enthusiastic, relaxed, energetic and smiley. It is important to make as much eye contact during the lecture as you can: if you have started the process advocated in the Enhanced Module of getting to know your students as soon as possible, you should feel their warmth helping you to overcome your nervousness.

A good strategy is to try to forget about yourself: think of how much you love your subject and how exciting it will be if you can convey understanding of it to your students so that they, too, feel engaged by it and curious to know more. Alternatively, if the lecture is one where you are intent upon making connections for the students, so that they will understand the overarching purposes of the module, remember how excited you felt in designing the module, and how exciting it will be for the students if you can convey an understanding of how all the pieces fit together. Avoid negative thoughts, because frankly no one wants to listen to a lecture given by someone who is negative and downbeat. Focus instead on the qualities that you are bringing to this particular party. They include:

- knowledge of your subject
- knowledge of how the module hangs together
- relevant material that you are presenting in a straightforward way
- encouragement
- enthusiasm
- interest in the students' progress.

Often our worries about lecturing crystallize around the first of these qualities and, particularly at the start of our careers, we feel that we 'don't know enough'. We may even feel like impostors. My answer to this, apart from the truism that we *are* all impostors to some extent, is four-fold and fairly pragmatic. First, no one can tell by looking at you or listening to you how much or how little you know. Second, however little you know, you surely know more than your students. Third, it is rather self-indulgent and precious to get hung up on the issue of whether or not you 'know enough'. You are not explaining the origins of the universe, just the application of some core concepts in your subject area, which you are presumably qualified to do. Fourth, and finally, no one can know absolutely everything about their subject, so if you get asked a question to which you don't know the answer, you can respond honestly and enthusiastically, as in 'What an interesting question! I really don't know the answer to that. You try to find out, and I will too, and we can discuss it next week.' (And make sure you *do* return to it the following week.)

Only the first two of the qualities listed above relates to your subject material – the other three are content-neutral and related to your commitment to the module and to your care for your students, and you will find that the more you focus on these aspects, the less you worry about your own deficiencies. It can help to remind yourself of the very worst speaker you know, and how much you would hate to sound like that person, and then visualize the best role model you know, and pretend to be that confident person for the space of the lecture hour. The funny thing about confidence is that if you pretend to have it in modest amounts, it does increase.

Another good strategy is to tell your students what your danger points or weaknesses are, and ask them to stop you if you indulge in them. So, you could say, 'When I get carried away, I talk too fast and go off at a tangent. If I do this, please call out "You're speeding!" ' If you admit to weaknesses, your audience will warm to you and, again, you will feel their warmth and support.

However, with all that said, it is unfortunately the case that many of us in recent years have noticed a somewhat different kind of response from students on occasion. In my own institution and at conferences, staff have reported a decline in courtesy among student audiences, and a tendency during lectures to engage in texting, chatting and messing around. This presents us with a problem, especially if we have worked hard at the cooperative model of teaching and learning that is at the heart of the Enhanced Module. It is tempting to switch into autocratic mode and demand silence and attention, but this would completely destroy the mood, as well as the implicit contract that you have tried to set up.

It is important to avoid irritation by remembering that this disrupting behaviour is probably not personally directed at you and does not imply a lack of respect. It may very well arise from short attention spans and the inability to handle the cognitive input of someone else talking for one hour. It may reflect other problems on the part of the students that just happen to manifest themselves in this particular way. You may redouble your efforts to make the lectures interactive, with no result. You may pause and wait meaningfully for the interruption to subside, or switch into an activity, only to have it start again as soon as you resume speaking.

In such a case, the best approach is to talk to the students involved, on a one-to-one basis, and ask each of them if they are enjoying the module and if they are having any problems in relation to any aspect of it. One or more may admit to a problem, such as undiagnosed dyslexia, a severe attention deficit or feeling convinced that they are on the wrong course. When they have admitted to a problem, you can offer help and appropriate support.

If they do not admit to having any problems, you can then say something like, 'I've noticed how hard you find it to concentrate in lectures – it must be very frustrating for you and I'm wondering how we can help you.' In this way, you are opening discussion of the issue as a problem for them, not for you, and this approach will not jeopardize the cooperative relationship you have worked so hard to set up. Later in the discussion, when the student has hopefully identified and described the problem, you can gently alert them to the distraction that their behaviour is posing for other students.

In terms of breaking up the lecture, you will have planned some short activities that test understanding. It is a good idea to drop these into the lecture just as you sense that concentration is waning. Very few of us can maintain our concentration in listening to a speaker for more than 15 or 20 minutes, so you should probably have three activities within a lecture.

In our subject of criminology, a useful activity is to put up on the overhead a slide of an ambiguous interpersonal situation, and ask the students to brainstorm for two minutes in pairs what exactly is going on. Dialogues in pairs or threes are a good activity, either where the students test each other on the understanding of key concepts, or provide three characteristics of an example, or recount a real-life example demonstrating a core claim. Getting students on their feet for these dialogic pairs is refreshing for them. After they have settled down, you can retest their understanding by asking them open questions, or giving them two statements and asking them to vote with a show of hands on the truth or falsity of each.

Delivery principles for lectures

- Get yourself in the mood by your favourite method.
- Keep the tone of lectures light, confident, enthusiastic and relaxed.
- Stick to your plan.
- State the message of each lecture, deliver that message, check understanding and re-state.
- Break up the one-hour slot with activities, such as paired dialogues, brainstorming and picture quizzes.

Evaluation and conclusion

Lectures often seem an outdated form of communication in today's interactive college or university. Given the choice, we might well have used the time very differently, but timetabling and room allocation are not issues over which we have control, and sometimes these constraints can act as barriers to change.

Lectures are not traditionally popular: in terms of enjoyment, our lectures were highly rated by 45% of students. Sometimes students would single out lectures as their 'best' aspect, citing their fascination, relevance or helpfulness in putting together the map of the module.

However, it is worth observing that, in lectures, it is hard to please all the people all the time. In one cycle, we felt that we had really got the activities in place in lectures and achieved the necessary lightness of touch. At the halfway point, we issued our mini-questionnaire on the best/worst aspects of the course so far. Many students cited the lectures, and the lecture breaks and activities in particular, as the best aspect. One student, however, identified 'lecture breaks' as the worst aspect, adding the remark 'Why can't we finish lectures ten minutes earlier by missing out all the breaks and activities?'

The mini-questionnaire, without doubt, kept our feet on the ground, maintained humility and showed us the need to work even harder to overcome the resistance of those who so far were not wholly engaged.

15

Enjoyment, self-awareness and reflection on feedback

Introduction

This chapter discusses the association between learning and enjoyment, and provides evidence about the different features of the Enhanced Module that students found enjoyable. There then follows some detail about our attempts to encourage private reflection and promote self-awareness about strengths and weaknesses. We consider the evidence of the sixth piece of assessment, which required students to reflect on the feedback they had received. The themes that recurred consistently during the four cycles are summarized, and some extracts in students' own words are reproduced to show how they were making sense of the feedback they had received, and were beginning to internalize and articulate an awareness of their own strengths and weaknesses. The chapter concludes by pointing out the advantages in our taking the long view – first, because it can take time for student reflection to come to fruition and, second, because it is an excellent antidote to professional discouragement.

Learning and enjoyment

Many students in further and higher education embark on the study of a discipline that they have never encountered before, and they are sometimes uncomfortable when they find that they are learning alongside students with, apparently, some substantial experience of the discipline through prior study. Sometimes they use this discomfort to further entrench their anxiety, on the grounds that these other students will do so much better than them. The reality is, of course, that all the students will be experiencing some anxiety, and the levels may well depend upon personal experiences in school, in the family and in previous assessments, rather than objective factors such as prior knowledge of the subject.

We have seen evidence earlier in this book about the levels of anxiety of our students, which tended to be overtly concentrated on the topic of assessment. In part this is because they perceive assessment as a judgement on them and their worth, and because the assessment experience has itself induced anxiety in the past.

But although their anxiety seems concentrated on this structured and definable part of future experience, they are actually experiencing a generalized and free-floating anxiety about the whole business of learning. They have left their comfort zone, in terms of the conceptualization of what is knowledge, how to reason and problem-solve, and how to express themselves verbally and in writing. In the social sciences, for example, they have to learn that the emphasis is on evidence-based writing, and that unsubstantiated opinions or claims are not valued.

It is a truism from developmental psychology that children learn through play: adults may find it harder to shed their inhibitions and their fear of 'looking silly', but the principle remains the same. Having fun makes us relax and more likely to open ourselves up to new learning experiences: it dispels the anxiety that in its extreme form is crippling. Anxiety can prevent us from relating to others in the group; it can prevent us from concentrating in lectures and seminars, and it can blinker us from recognizing our own progress. When feedback is delivered, the anxious self may hear the critical tone, but without registering the praise and constructive suggestions. The anxious self may register 'I am not good enough – again.'

So, from the outset of the module, we did our best to assuage this corrosive anxiety. This was the rationale behind the intensity of our efforts to break the ice at the outset of the module, to deliver a class test that was non-threatening and stimulating, and to deliver a module programme containing activities that embodied learning through fun.

If the learning experience is an enjoyable one, not only will anxiety be further reduced, but there is a greater likelihood that students will be better able to reflect on their learning, and learn more from feedback. Our little mantra 'Feedback, feed forward' was a constant reminder to us to couch our personalized remarks on the feedback sheet in terms of how the student could use this feedback in the next assessment task.

In the first and second cycles of the Enhanced Module, I observed the fun that students got out of the icebreakers, many of the learning activities and the outside visits. I even began to suspect that they were enjoying assessments.

So, in the third and fourth cycles, a section was added to the post-module questionnaire, listing seven different aspects of the module and asking students to rate how much they had enjoyed them on a scale of 1 to 5, where 1 was 'Not enjoyable at all', and 5 was 'Highly enjoyable'.

There were no ratings of 1 ('Not enjoyable at all') for any item from any student. The worst results were ratings of 2, which were given by 20% of students to 'Relevant reading', by 7.5% of students to 'Lectures', and by 2.5% of students to 'Outside visits' and 'Feedback'.

Overwhelmingly, enjoyment rates were high, as the following figures show:

	Ratings of 4 or 5 awarded by % of students
Outside visits	85%
Seminar activities	72.5%
'Double act' co-teaching	70%
Feedback	60%
Assessments	57.5%
Lectures	45%
Relevant reading	25%

It was clear that our attempts to make learning enjoyable had been successful. It was not surprising that outside visits, seminar activities and the 'double act' were rated so highly, because the palpable 'buzz' from students in relation to these aspects was overt. The high enjoyment ratings for feedback from 60% of students were pleasing because feedback itself does involve constructive criticism, and this is not always a wholly enjoyable experience for the recipient.

However, the enjoyment ratings that most surprised and pleased us were those for assessments, which do not normally rank as favourite activities for students. Well over half of them had rated assessments highly in terms of enjoyment. What was even more exciting, when asked to say in their own words what was the single *best* thing and single *worst* thing about the module, 12.5% declared assessments to be the single *best* thing. More predictably, 10% of students declared assessments as the single *worst* thing.

Enjoyment not only facilitates understanding, it helps students to bond with their group and feel a sense of integration in their course. My parallel research with students who had withdrawn from the institution had revealed that this lack of a sense of integration and 'belongingness' with their cohort had contributed to their withdrawal. So, in the third cycle of the Enhanced Module, a question was added to the post-module questionnaire, which asked students to say whether the module had helped them settle in, or bond with, their group. Here is how they responded:

- 60% said that the module had helped a lot to settle them into, or bond with, their group.
- 32.5% said that it had helped a little.
- 5% said that it had made no difference.

Encouraging self-awareness

Our intuition was that, by Christmas, students were sufficiently settled in to an enjoyable learning experience to tackle issues of self-awareness. By then, everyone had experienced individual and group feedback in both written and oral forms, and we had worked hard at building self-esteem. This was the point at which we had a seminar activity that included use of the self-awareness quiz (see Appendix 5). This took place in seminar time, and students were advised that they could write all over it and use any system of their own choosing in completing it. They could of course give themselves scores for each question, but we did not suggest this because we did not want to present the quiz to them as something with a quantitative outcome. It was designed to provoke thought as to their own participation. Since they were only halfway through the module, it might perhaps stimulate some of them to change their attitudes or habits in a positive way. As a researcher I longed to know how they completed it, but as their lecturer I had to assure them of absolute freedom and anonymity. The document was solely for their use and their records.

Something like this is a slow burner, and designed to settle in thought, perhaps being revisited on occasion. It was, we hoped, a bridge to the sixth piece of assessment, which required students, in seminar time, to sit with their portfolio of work and feedback, and reflect on their learning experiences.

Reflection on feedback

The sixth piece of assessment required students to reflect on the module, on all the feedback they had received, on their strengths and weaknesses, and on how they felt that they learned best. It carried only 10% of overall marks, and it was stressed to students that marks would be awarded on the relevance of their reflection in relation to the specifics of their own learning, not on whether they praised or criticized the module. In relation to reflecting on the module, the following were recurrent themes expressed in students' own words:

- 'Exceptional enjoyment'
- 'Exciting learning'
- 'Marking my work so I can see where the marks come from'
- 'Seeing myself improve'
- 'Setting myself higher standards now'
- 'Realizing my ability'
- 'Aiming to show my true potential in the second year'
- 'Realizing that deadlines do matter'
- 'Why aren't other modules like this?'

In terms of criticism, they often commented constructively on the organizational details of the outside visit to Parliament, which was extremely demanding to arrange. In relation to feedback, the following themes were common, again in students' own words:

- 'Turning my weaknesses into strengths'
- 'Applying feedback to my other modules'
- 'Helping me track my progress'
- 'Encouraging me to be consistent'
- 'Rewarding my effort'
- 'Helping me re-evaluate my work'
- 'Increased my confidence'

Particularly pleasing also was the fact that, at some level, after all the varied activities and assessments on the Enhanced Module, all these first-level students were reflecting constructively about how they learn best, as the following quotations show:

'I feel I learn best when I am told to research and write an assignment in class with all my notes to hand. This was reflected in my grade. My consistent weakness in other assignments has been not including background research, a range of sources and a bibliography. I feel that by having this type of module structure with regular assessments, it helps students to gradually progress. The advice you receive after each assessment is really useful. I find the front sheet to each assessment particularly useful as the marking scheme is in front of the student.'

'I have finally discovered my own learning style through this module. Every assignment taught me something new. I learn best through reading the materials given by the tutor and then finding my own sources of information, usually with the help of the module bibliography. I also learn a lot from lectures as they point me in the right direction as to what information I should be reading. My weakness in terms of learning skills is my absolute hatred of the internet. This hampers my research technique because I am not making full use of the range of sources. I do not like using the internet for information because I find its validity questionable, and I would rather read a good textbook or journal that I know to be reputable than waste valuable hours searching the web only to end up with a few pages of useful work.'

'This module put me on a learning curve in terms of how I research assignments, make observations, style my writing, analyse and summarize my research, and how to use feedback to my advantage. I now plan my assignments much more carefully, allowing for plenty of time to research information and edit final drafts before submission. I also think very carefully about the way I word my sentences so that they are concise and meaningful, rather than long-winded and often irrelevant.'

Many students commented favourably on the support they had received in the module in response to their needs. However, it was also clear that even those students who had not needed extra support had appreciated a supportive learning environment, as the following remark shows:

'Although I have not felt the need for any support throughout the module, I have been very aware of [tutor's name] presence. Having the support of the lecturer makes a difference, as in many other modules they do not know your name, and the personalization of this module makes it a lot less formal.'

Another pleasing aspect of student reflection was that very many had confronted and acknowledged their weaknesses:

'The trip to Parliament was exhausting because you had to rely on your powers of observation and memory alone. This piece of work was the hardest to complete and had the lowest mark. *On reflection I should have written the report that day*, but with reference guides, the internet and leaflets I was able to complete it.' (emphasis added)

'The ratings that I have received for referencing have improved between Assignment 1 and Assignment 4. The constant feedback that I have received after each assignment has allowed me to pinpoint my weaknesses and attempt to improve them.'

'When looking back over the module, I realize if I had put a little more effort into proofreading my work, then my grades might have been better. My grades have been low. My structure and coherence have got worse.'

Many students mentioned the connection with their other modules:

'[The first assessment] helped me to improve the finding of relevant sources and with practice from doing background research, I extrapolated this technique to other aspects of my course.'

Perhaps one of the recurrent themes most welcome to us was that of increased confidence:

'In the past I have always been afraid of the subject I am writing about, and that I will completely lose the plot of my work. With this module I have improved, I have become more confident of what I'm writing, and have stuck to the subject matter. This may have something to do with the assignments . . . and the field trips, which brought us face to face with what we had to write about.'

Sometimes increased confidence came about as a result of realizing personal competence at particular skills:

'From the Houses of Parliament visit, I think my listening and observing skills are good. We had to remember everything as paper was not permitted. My analysing skills may not be so good. I think I have improved my writing skills since the first assignment. My paragraphing has let me down but my spelling has helped me. I learn best from listening to others. I also learn well from reading books.'

However, the messages of feedback did not always result in the immediate achievement of the desired result. A student who had persistently been offered extra help with a study skills support tutor still had not taken this up by the end of the module. He had found another solution:

'ƒor my first two piece of work I was continually *pointed out about* spelling and *grammer*, so for my third piece I made sure that it was a very good piece of work. I got other people to proof *reed* it and help with *grammer* and spelling. Which made a *Big* difference *Because thier* was a *Big* improvement in my work [sic].'

I tracked the student who wrote these comments through his three-year degree programme. He eventually graduated with a third-class degree, and told me that if the Enhanced Module had not been so encouraging, he would have dropped out in his first year. He said it had shown him that, although he had great weaknesses, he could succeed if he persevered. He said that he did his best to use feedback positively and took advantage of all the help that was on offer, eventually signing up with the study skills support service at the start of his second year, after an internal struggle over whether or not he should seek such help. It is very hard for some students to accept that they need help, and to take the initiative in seeking it.

Conclusion

Over the four years, we encountered many anecdotal stories from students who in their second or third years claimed that the Enhanced Module had prevented them from withdrawing from university in their first year. These anecdotes do not constitute evidence of the module's success, but they were certainly moving endorsements of the results of the more systematized evaluation. They showed us that some of our innovations were indeed like slow fuses that we had lit in the sensibilities of our students. Additionally, they shored up our enthusiasm and commitment, for we could never rule out the possibility that our support would not prove significant, if not now then at some point in the future, and this possibility was grounds for remaining enthusiastic, persistent and optimistic in our practice.

16

Evaluation and continued enhancement

It is clear from the fundamental principles I have described that the Enhanced Module was intended to be enriched so as to include a great deal of overt support, skills practice, encouragement and flexibility in response to student needs. But all this effort would have been pointless had the processes of evaluation and subsequent modification not been part of the project. It was vital to assess the impact of the module using as many evaluation tools as possible. The following list summarizes the evaluation tools that I have already indicated were used over the four cycles:

- the pre-module questionnaire (see Appendix 7)
- the halfway enquiry into best/worst aspects (see Appendix 8)
- the post-module questionnaire (see Appendix 9)
- the post-module focus group by lecturers or independent researchers
- registers
- overall grades
- self-reflection by tutors
- dialogue between tutors
- dialogue with students.

For all our questionnaires and focus groups, the principles of anonymity and confidentiality were emphasized. Since these were social science students, they were either already familiar with questionnaires as a form of enquiry, or receptive as to their intentions, and did not experience any difficulties with the 5-point scale. With students from other disciplines, it could be profitable to do a little preparation with them before completion of the questionnaire, so that they take it seriously.

The pre-module questionnaire (Appendix 7) was administered in the very first lecture, prior even to the module programme being given out, and was presented to students as a routine general enquiry unrelated to this module in particular. The halfway enquiry into best/worst aspects (Appendix 8) was completed in the last seminar before the Christmas break. The post-module questionnaire (Appendix 9) was administered in the same seminar as the sixth assessment, the reflection on feedback, when students were already in a reflective mode of thought.

The focus groups were generally held in the last few weeks of the module, when an independent researcher would show up unannounced during a seminar and the module tutors would leave the room. We generally managed to get the Student Union to provide an independent researcher, and she had the advantage of being known to the students, but in a social context entirely unrelated to their learning. We felt that had they major or minor criticisms, they would not have been inhibited about expressing them. In one cycle, she was coincidentally undertaking the monitoring of the student experience on a diet of wholly conventional modules, and the contrast between her results for the conventional diet and the Enhanced Module was striking. The criticisms and complaints for the diet of conventional modules were in strong contrast to the appreciation for the Enhanced Module.

Analysis of the registers told us that the attendance levels on this module were much higher than for conventional modules. The pass rate was always higher than on conventional modules, but by the fourth cycle we had improved and refined many aspects of the module and achieved a 100% pass rate. The module had initially been designed in response to student criticism of their learning environment, so naturally our strongest focus in terms of evaluation was on the considered judgements of students themselves.

The results of the questionnaires, the focus groups and other evidence show that the research questions in Chapter 1 were met with affirmative answers.

- Student anxiety about assessment in general was considerably diminished.
- Attitudes towards attendance and attendance levels were changed positively.
- Enjoyment levels were high and the learning outcomes were achieved.
- Students reflected on their progress in constructive ways.
- Outside visits were integrated into the whole learning experience.

But this was not a result that meant we could sit back with satisfaction and prepare to deliver the module in exactly the same format all over again. Evaluation without change would have been sterile. 'Enhancement' is a dynamic principle, and the following section details some instances of continuity of enhancement in response to student concerns.

Continuous enhancement

From the very first cycle, students made criticisms of aspects that they did not like, and suggestions as to possible improvements, and, where appropriate, these were incorporated into the next cycle. Their feedback therefore fed into the ongoing enhancement process.

Three examples will show how the enhancement of the module itself was cumulative as a result of student feedback. The first example concerns the often-repeated comments by students in the first two cycles that they needed help with the specific skill of note-taking in lectures; some added the comment that they had never before experienced the lecture format, and that their previous teachers in school or college had taught solely by the provision of handouts. Others commented that the skill of note-taking in lectures, which they found so difficult, was not overtly related to a graded assessment, and that this had a poor effect on their motivation during lectures. Even with the best of intentions, they tended to abandon their note-taking, lose concentration and 'drift'.

Our solution to this concern is linked to the second example. In individual reflection, and in our shared reflections, we had to face the fact that we still had a long way to go to achieve lectures that were truly student-centred. In our halfway best/worst feedback questionnaire, some students cited 'boring lectures' as the 'worst thing', and the truth of this criticism was not mitigated by other students pronouncing them 'fascinating'. In the third cycle, therefore, an even more determined effort was made to make lectures more student-centred. The detail of this is covered in Chapter 14.

Nevertheless, we remained aware that, throughout their degree programme, they would have to cope with traditional teacher-centred lectures, and effective note-taking was a useful skill both for this and in the world of employment. So, additionally, students were given explicit guidance and encouragement about different styles of note-taking, and were required, as part of one of their formal assessments, to produce for inspection their entire lecture notes for the module at the end of the year. This requirement also fed into our emphasis on full attendance.

The third example relates to expressed student concerns about different experiences depending on which of the two tutors was in charge of their particular seminar group. It should be noted that the tutors had very different teaching styles, even though they wholeheartedly shared the philosophy and goals of the Enhanced Module. For the third and fourth cycle, then, seminar groups were rolled together so that both tutors attended every seminar, and, in addition, every lecture. This had the effect of setting up a dialogue between the tutors, and of demonstrating that there could be contrasting views on particular topics, each with evidence to back it up. When, at the halfway point in the third cycle, a mini-questionnaire asked students in an entirely open question to identify the 'best' and 'worst' aspects of the module so far, 80% spontaneously identified what had become known as 'the double act' as the 'best' aspect.

This best/worst mini-questionnaire (see Appendix 8) was administered just before the Christmas break, and it provided us with ammunition, even during an actual cycle of the module, to feed back student perceptions into our practice. It also functioned as a source of encouragement to us, at a time when we were finding the rigours of the module demanding. Apart from the teaching double act, best aspects for students were invariably other issues of teaching style, the provision of feedback or general support. For 'worst' aspects, about 20% of students would identify aspects of their own performance, such as time management or levels of attendance. We found it encouraging that some students were beginning to be reflective about their own input and practice.

There were always students who mentioned timetabling issues as the 'worst' aspect but, as we explained to them, the timetable was outside our control. Some students would single out individual aspects of content that they did not like, so this was our cue to try harder to show the relevance of these to the overall picture.

Another interesting criticism, only ever from one or two students, was that our feedback focused on the structure of work rather than on the content. This struck a chord with us. It seemed particularly true on those occasions when the most able students submitted work that did not require any correction to structure, conceptualization, style, expression and organization.

It is clearly not satisfactory if, in a student cohort embodying great diversity, the most able feel disregarded. We resolved in future to pay particular attention during general and individual feedback to discussing content, and suggesting further and more challenging reading where appropriate. We discussed the formation of a reading group to which such students could come, but resources did not permit this, and cautious voices expressed the fear that such a move could be divisive.

I still see this as a potential weakness in our practice, however, to which one solution could be the formation of a student-led society that would take the initiative in exploring deeper aspects of a discipline, and to which staff could voluntarily contribute. Such societies are an integral part of older universities that do not reflect widening participation to such a great extent, but they are not, to my knowledge, common in the newer universities and institutes of higher education. In part, this reflects how very stretched our diverse students are in attempting to balance paid work, timetabled classes and family responsibilities.

17
Conclusion

This book has provided an overview of a rich project, which brought staff and students closer together so as to foster student understanding and a sense of integration in their studies. In terms of richness, it has to be stressed how many small yet immeasurable encounters there were between students and tutors that showed us how appreciative the students were of the huge efforts we made to support and encourage them. In the jargon, these would come under the heading of 'personal support', but they were so very much more than that. They were like gold nuggets of nurture that accrued over the course of a year, serving to improve self-confidence and binding students into a fully integrated learning experience.

Personal support, both in terms of learning and personal issues, is recognized throughout the literature as crucial to student success, whether it is provided by teachers, specialists or peers (see Romainville and Noel (1998) for a discussion of the different types). Importantly, in this module, personal support really was personal, and it was stitched right through the module content, frequent assessment, a lively and supportive learning environment, and the provision of individual feedback.

The issues of assessment and feedback are, however, equally important as ingredients of personal and intellectual support. As Rust (2002) notes, the research literature points to the value of clearly articulated assessment practices coupled with effective feedback. To this I would add that, on the evidence of this project, assessment can even become a favourite activity for students who are properly integrated into an enjoyable learning experience.

In brief summary, the findings show that the research questions posed earlier were well met by this Enhanced Module. Assessment anxiety was reduced by the experience of the module. This demanding type of portfolio assessment turned out to be a favourite for the large majority of students, and the fact that by the third cycle every student completed a portfolio and passed the module indicated that the learning outcomes were achieved. It was absolutely clear from the evidence that students had largely enjoyed the module and found it enormously supportive. It had certainly produced a high degree of self-reflection about personal learning styles, motivation and achievement. The outside visits were an integral part of the module curriculum and assessment strategy, and repeatedly comments on the post-module questionnaires indicated that students enjoyed and benefited from seeing for themselves the workings of power and criminal justice.

What had not been fully anticipated was the extent of enjoyment and enthusiasm produced by this module. In focus groups, the quality of student appreciation was overwhelming. Students did indeed enjoy their studies, become conscious of progress and increased self-confidence, and reflect on their own learning in constructive ways. A frequently reiterated question was this: why could not all modules be like this one?

The experience of having a colleague to 'bounce off' produced a much livelier atmosphere in seminars, and seemed to melt the usual inhibitions of first-year students, encouraging them to debate issues in a more adventurous way. Because we two lecturers disagreed on occasion, and were prepared to bring forward evidence to support our assertions, students were able to see how concepts function in essentially contestable ways in the human sciences.

It is vital to point out that this experiment in joined-up learning and joined-up fun was not only enhancing for students. The pay-off for us as teachers was also considerable: delivery of this kind of learning experience made us feel valued and valuable. There was a palpable air of excitement and involvement in our seminars, and if we ever entered them slightly frazzled and weary, it is fair to say that we always left on a high. It is true that much extra work was involved, especially in relation to marking and providing personalized feedback within one week of hand in for each task. Front loading the first-level experience must therefore take into account staff resources and the extra time required for delivery of Enhanced Modules of this type. From the evidence of this project, it can be argued that:

- all students should do *one* Enhanced Module at the first and second levels.
- extra resources should be provided to design and deliver Enhanced Modules.
- resources can be vired from the third-year teaching budget, because by then students will have developed into much more independent learners.

Enhanced Modules of this type, which use a range of strategies (Johnston 2001) in a planned and integrated way, are a vital tool in maximizing student participation, achievement and retention: they should be constantly evaluated in the kind of research feedback loop demonstrated here, in order to keep the learning experience responsive to the ever-widening needs of a diverse range of students.

Appendix 1: attendance support policy

We want you to succeed on this module. One of the keys to your success is regular attendance at all lectures and seminars, and this policy is designed to help you achieve that. There are things that we expect from you, and things that we will provide for you.

We expect:

- that you will attend and participate in every lecture or seminar unless you have good reason to be absent
- that you will tell us your reason in advance if you cannot attend a lecture or seminar
- that you will tell us your reason afterwards if you were unable to attend and unable to give us prior warning.

In return, we assure you:

- that every lecture and seminar matters, and they all relate to your learning and success on this module
- that you can contact us at any time by text, telephone or email
- that we will record your attendance consistently
- that we will reward you for excellent attendance
- that we will follow up unexplained absences sympathetically
- that we will offer support when attendance is difficult for you
- that we will help you to catch up if poor attendance has hampered your progress
- that we will penalize you if you do not attend and you are unable to provide a valid reason either before or after the event.

To text or telephone, please use this number: _____

To email, please use this address: _____

Appendix 2: attendance support – enquiry into absence

Dear _____

We have missed seeing you in classes, and wonder what is preventing you from attending. As you know, we have a very active policy of supporting attendance in this module, so we really want to know if we can help in any way.

If you feel worried because you think you may have dropped behind, we would like to meet with you and help you to catch up.

Please get in touch either by letter, email or text, and let us know what is happening with you. Remember, we want you to enjoy your studies!

Looking forward to seeing you or hearing from you.

With best wishes,

_____

Contact details

Telephone: _____

Text: _____

Email: _____

Appendix 3: assignment feedback form

(NB: The values in columns would change as criteria and weight of each criteria change.)
Student name:
Module title:
Module code:
Assignment title:

Please asterisk any items below on which you want detailed feedback and advice

Criteria	Weight	Excellent 8.33	Good 6.66	Satisfactory 5.0	Fair 3.33	Poor 1.66
Overall presentation		☐	☐	☐	☐	☐
Structure and coherence		☐	☐	☐	☐	☐
Evidence of research		☐	☐	☐	☐	☐
Consistent attention to question		☐	☐	☐	☐	☐
Demonstrating understanding and insight		☐	☐	☐	☐	☐
Providing context and background		☐	☐	☐	☐	☐
Grammar and sentence structure		☐	☐	☐	☐	☐
Spelling		☐	☐	☐	☐	☐
Paragraphing and punctuation		☐	☐	☐	☐	☐
Relevance and range of sources		☐	☐	☐	☐	☐
Citations within text (Surname, year: page)		☐	☐	☐	☐	☐
Referencing in Bibliography		☐	☐	☐	☐	☐

(*continued overleaf*)

Strengths:

Weaknesses:

Things we will talk about at a one-to-one:

Further comments

Percentage mark: . . . .

NB: All marks are provisional until confirmed by a formally constituted Board of Examiners.

Signed: . . . .

Date of marking: . . . .

Appendix 4: example of a team collaboration activity

Designing a prison – instructions for students

Our overall task over three weeks is to plan a new prison, the chief aim of which is to reduce reoffending. The following principles apply:

- it must be run within the law
- it will be inspected regularly by external authorities
- it must be capable of housing 500 young male offenders (18 to 21)
- it must have an imaginative regime dedicated to the main aim of reducing reoffending
- except for diet (see below) your budget is open-ended.

As one of the members of the working party in charge of this prison, we want you to assume that you will be financially liable for each and every inmate who reoffends within two years of release, over and above the 25% mark. As soon as the reoffending rate reaches 35%, you can assume for the purposes of this exercise that you will yourself be incarcerated in the prison for three months and subjected to the same regime as the other inmates.

The inmates have been sentenced for periods of up to four years, for crimes ranging from drugs offences to violent assault (excluding sexual offences and murder). Some are illiterate, many have been brought up in care, have poor social and coping skills, and seriously self-harm. Some are vulnerable, some are habitual bullies.

Group 1

Your task is to design and produce a plan of a prison on A3 squared paper (provided), showing all the buildings, the space between buildings and the perimeter.

Group 2

Your task is to devise the overall regime. Please produce a timetable for the inmates for the week (some days may be the same, some not). It should include out-of-cell activities such as work, education, sport and any other features that you think will help fulfil the aim of reducing reoffending on release.

Group 3

Your task is to design healthcare, diet and education, all of which will operate entirely within the prison. Your budget for feeding the inmates is £1 per head per day – sample menus please!

Group 4

Like all well-run institutions, this prison has rules. Your task is to write the rulebook for the prison, and specify the penalties for breaking the rules. You will need to devise a way of monitoring punishment and safeguarding prisoner well-being during punishment.

Groups will need to have preliminary discussions among themselves, and then consult other groups, since the work of each group affects all other groups. For instance, the plans cannot be drawn without knowledge of the requirements that arise from the type of regime, decisions about health and education, a knowledge of the rules and penalties, etc.

Groups are advised that they will need to do library and internet research between meetings, and they should divide what needs to be done between members of the group. As far as possible, this work should be done in pairs.

Appendix 5: self-awareness quiz

Dear Student,

This form is entirely confidential and just for your own records, so you can write on it exactly as you wish. No one will see it except *you*.

The following questions remind you of some of the skills that your first-level modules have revolved around, so that you can consider to what extent you have developed these skills and what still remains to be done. We all find it difficult to face up to our own weaknesses, and sometimes it can help if we do so in writing, safe in the knowledge that no one else is ever going to see it.

By the end of the first year, you should have taken some steps towards becoming an independent learner. This is shorthand for several differences to the kind of learner you were at school or college, where you probably had people chasing you up about tasks and deadlines. This does not happen in higher education. An independent learner is more mature and responsible. He/she does not expect or want to be 'spoon-fed'. He/she takes charge of his/her own learning, uses his/her initiative, takes all steps necessary to find out the characteristics and demands of the chosen course, and complies punctually with all requirements. So, for example, an independent learner:

- sets themselves goals, and is able to carry them out, without being nagged or reminded over and over again
- manages their time effectively; prepares in advance for coursework or seminar activities; hands in assignments on time
- takes notice of feedback, and learns from it; faces up to constructive criticism and acts on it
- learns to identify their own learning style, and strengths and weaknesses; takes steps to improve weaknesses, attending skills support classes if these are available, or seeking help with literacy and numeracy problems.

You may have thought of other examples in the exercise we have just done in class.

Here are some questions to get you thinking about your self-development in relation to the modules you have studied so far. You could write 'Yes', 'No' or 'Sometimes' beside them, where relevant, or use ticks and crosses.

Time management

- Have I organized my life so that I can attend all lectures and seminars regularly?
- Have I set aside some time each week, for each module, to do the necessary reading and preparation work?
- Have I handed in all my assignments on time?
- How soon (if ever) did I contact my MP, after the original instruction?
- If I have handed in an assignment or assignments late, what was the reason? With better time management, could this have been avoided?
- Do I rush from one thing to another, always feeling as if I am trying to 'catch up'? Do I have weeks where I just cannot fit everything in?

On a scale of 1 to 10, bearing in mind your answers to the above questions, circle the number that corresponds to how you rate *your* time-management skills:

Poor   1   2   3   4   5   6   7   8   9   10   Excellent

- Is this in any way an improvement since you came to university? If so, by how much? And what factor(s) has/have helped you improve?

Study skills

- On my feedback sheets, have I ever got critical comments or a low mark for sentence structure, punctuation, paragraphing, spelling, referencing, structure, and generally reading through and checking my work?
- If so, what have I done about it?

  (Write answer here)

- Have I gone to the skills support classes, or sought a one-to-one with my academic tutor or the skills support tutor? If not, why not?

  (Write reasons here)

- Have I got the necessary word-processing skills to turn out beautifully presented work, using spellcheck? If not, what have I done about it?

(Write answer here)

- Do I always take action following constructive feedback? If so, how?
- Have I ever had the same weakness pointed out in feedback more than once? If so, why did I not take notice of the feedback the first time?

In general terms, circle a score for how competent your overall study skills are:

Poor   1   2   3   4   5   6   7   8   9   10   Excellent

- Is this in any way an improvement since you came to university? If so, by how much? And what factor(s) has/have helped you improve?

Listening skills

Think about all the information you are given verbally, and try to answer the following questions.

- Do I always make a note of instructions I am given about deadlines and about course requirements?
- In seminars, when the tutor issues instructions and requests, do I grasp the information the first time I hear it?
- In group work, how good am I at listening to the other people in my group? Or am I just using the time when they speak to plan what I am going to say next?
- In lectures, do I remain focused and get the gist of the lecture written down in note form?

On a scale of 1 to 10, assess your listening skills:

Poor   1   2   3   4   5   6   7   8   9   10   Excellent

- Is this in any way an improvement since you came to university? If so, by how much? And what factor(s) has/have helped you improve?

Group work

Thinking back to the prison design exercise, and other group work you have done, try to consider if you have played a full part in the group, by answering the following questions.

- Did I make a point of introducing myself to people I didn't know, and asking them who they were?
- Have I been as confident as I would like?
- Have I made an effort to take the group work seriously, or have I just mucked about, trying to be funny and impress others?
- Have I dominated the talking?
- Have I remained silent and passive?
- Have I tried to draw out opinions from others less confident than myself?
- Have I pulled my weight in preparation for group-work tasks?

On a scale of 1 to 10, assess your group-work skills:

Poor   1   2   3   4   5   6   7   8   9   10   Excellent

- Is this in any way an improvement since you came to university? What do you think has helped you improve, or stopped you improving still further?

Goals

You might like to consider setting yourself one or two goals in relation to one or more of these skills. Keep them modest. If you achieve them, you can set some more. Make sure, however, that they are not *vague*. If you can measure them, you will know when you have achieved them. If you cannot measure them because they are too vague, how will you ever be able to pat yourself on the back for having achieved them?

Here are some examples of goals. The first column shows them in vague and imprecise form; the second column shows the same goals in an achievable form.

Vague goals (not much use!)	Achievable goals (useful!)
I will make more time for background reading	I will do an hour's background reading in my weakest module each week for six weeks
I will be more proactive in seminars	I will make at least one verbal contribution in every seminar activity
I will make more effort to understand lectures	I will ask the lecturer to explain whenever I don't understand something in a lecture.

Now set yourself a personal goal:

This form is for your personal records. Keep it and revisit it from time to time. You will be surprised how your skills improve over time. Good luck!

Appendix 6: end-of-module letter to students with poor attendance records

Dear _____

You have managed to successfully complete this module, but the records show that you have not attended consistently. This is one factor that has led to you submitting fewer pieces of work than you were asked to do. At the second level and beyond, this failure to submit would cause you to fail the module.

Please be aware that students with low levels of attendance on degree pro-grammes tend to have more problems than students who attend regularly, and this can lead to academic failure. It is very important to attend lectures and seminars regularly, so that you are fully aware of what you are being asked to do, and the deadlines for when you must hand in the work.

If you think that your attendance problems will continue, and you would like to talk to someone about the factors that are hindering your attendance, please contact me. I will be able to suggest some sources of support for you, which will help you progress in your studies. Remember, we want to help you to succeed, and to enjoy your studies.

With best wishes,

_____

Contact details:

Appendix 7: pre-module questionnaire

Dear Student,

Please answer the questions as honestly as you can, by ticking *one* of the answers provided. This questionnaire is absolutely anonymous. Thank you for your help.

1 **How anxious would you say you are about assessment *in general*?**
   - Not at all anxious
   - A little bit anxious
   - Moderately anxious
   - Very anxious
   - Extremely anxious

2 **How anxious would you say you are about *exams*?**
   - Not at all anxious
   - A little bit anxious
   - Moderately anxious
   - Very anxious
   - Extremely anxious

3 **How anxious would you say that you are about *assessed essays*?**
   - Not at all anxious
   - A little bit anxious
   - Moderately anxious
   - Very anxious
   - Extremely anxious

4 **How anxious would you say you are about *assessed presentations in seminars*?**
   - Not at all anxious
   - A little bit anxious
   - Moderately anxious
   - Very anxious
   - Extremely anxious

5   Please tick the form(s) of assessment that you would most prefer:
   • Examinations
   • Essays
   • Presentations in seminar
   • Short written tasks done in your own time
   • Short written tasks done in seminar time
   • A mix of several different types of task
   • Other (please explain)

6   How important do you think attendance is at *lectures*?
   • Not at all important
   • A little bit important
   • Moderately important
   • Very important
   • Extremely important

7   And how important do you think attendance is at *seminars*?
   • More important than for lectures
   • The same level of importance as for lectures
   • Less important than for lectures

8   On a scale of 1 to 10, how would you rate your motivation in general, as you begin your degree? (1 is extremely low, 10 is extremely high)

9   Can you, using your own words, describe what would help you to increase your motivation, *or*, if it is already high, what would help it to remain high?

10   On a scale of 1 to 10, as you begin your studies, how confident are you of graduating? (1 is extremely low, 10 is extremely high)

11   In your own words, please write what, if anything, would help to boost your confidence. If it is already high, what do you think will help to keep it high?

Appendix 8: best/worst mini-questionnaire

Dear Student,

We are halfway through the module! How about telling us about your experience of it so far? Please answer the following two questions as honestly as possible. Remember, this is completely confidential.

What has been the BEST aspect of this module so far for you?

What has been the WORST aspect of this module so far for you?

Appendix 9: post-module questionnaire

Dear Student,

Please choose one of the answers provided and tick it. This questionnaire is absolutely anonymous. Thank you for your help.

(a) **After your experience on this module, how anxious are you about assessment *in general*?**

 1 Not at all anxious
 2 A little bit anxious
 3 Moderately anxious
 4 Very anxious
 5 Extremely anxious

(b) **So are you *less* anxious about assessment in general than you were at the start of the module, or *more* anxious?**

 1 Less anxious
 2 More anxious
 3 No change

(c) **Please number the following forms of assessment in your order of preference, using a scale of 1 to 5, so that:**
Your *least* favourite = 1   2   3   4   5 = your *most* favourite

 1 Examination
 2 One long essay or two/three shorter essays
 3 Presentations in seminar
 4 A mix of tasks spread over the module (i.e. the form of portfolio assessment we use on this module)
 5 Other (please specify)

(d) **Have you found the *spoken* feedback (given either in class or to you individually) helpful in this module?**

 1 Not at all helpful
 2 A little bit helpful
 3 Moderately helpful

4 Very helpful

5 Extremely helpful

(e) **Have you found the *written* feedback given to you helpful in this module?**

1 Not at all helpful

2 A little bit helpful

3 Moderately helpful

4 Very helpful

5 Extremely helpful

(f) **Can you describe in your own words one way in which feedback has helped you *personally*?**

(g) **As part of your learning and development, how important do you think feedback is?**

1 Not at all important

2 A little bit important

3 Moderately important

4 Very important

5 Extremely important

(h) **As part of your learning and development, how important do you think it is for you to take notice of the feedback you have been given?**

1 Not at all important

2 A little bit important

3 Moderately important

4 Very important

5 Extremely important

(i) **Has the fact that assessments were spread throughout the module affected your attendance in any way?**

1 It has encouraged my attendance

2 It has discouraged my attendance

3 It has made no difference to my attendance pattern

(j) Have you received any enquiries about non-attendance?

1 Yes
2 No

If yes, did you find the enquiry supportive?

1 Yes (please say why):

2 No (please say why not):

(k) We have taught as a 'double act', with both tutors present all of
the time. On a scale of 1 to 5, how helpful has the 'double act' been
to your learning? Please circle the appropriate number:

Not at all helpful   1   2   3   4   5   Extremely helpful

(l) We would like to know how *enjoyable* you have found the different
aspects of this module. Please look at the following items below and
circle the relevant number:

Not at all enjoyable 1   2   3   4   5   Extremely enjoyable

Lectures	1 2 3 4 5
Seminar activities	1 2 3 4 5
The teaching 'double act'	1 2 3 4 5
Trips to court and Parliament	1 2 3 4 5
Assessment tasks	1 2 3 4 5
The feedback	1 2 3 4 5
Relevant reading	1 2 3 4 5

(m) Do you think that, over the course of the year, this module has helped
you in any way settle in, or bond with, your group?

1 It has helped a lot
2 It has helped a little
3 It has not made any difference.

If it has helped you at all, can you say how?

(n) On a scale of 1 to 5, how supportive have you found the tutors on this module?

Not at all supportive   1   2   3   4   5   Extremely supportive

(o) What has been the *best* thing about this module, for you?

(p) What has been the *worst* thing about this module, for you?

If you have other comments, please add them here:

References

Berg, B.L. (2008) *Qualitative Research Methods for the Social Sciences* (7th edn). Boston, MA: Allyn & Bacon.

Biggs, J. (2003) *Teaching for Quality Learning at University* (2nd edn). Buckingham: SRHE and Open University Press.

BNU (2008) *Students in Human Sciences 2003–2006, Internal Statistics*. High Wycombe: Buckinghamshire New University.

Brown, S. and Knight, P. (1994) *Assessing Learners in Higher Education*. London: Kogan Page.

Brown, S. with Bull, J. and Pendlebury, M. (1997) *Assessing Student Learning in Higher Education*. London: Routledge.

Corradi Fiumara, G. (1990) *The Other Side of Language: A Philosophy of Listening*. London: Routledge

Gibbs, G. (1992) *Improving the Quality of Student Learning*. Bristol: TES.

Gibbs, G. (1999) 'Using assessment strategically to change the ways students learn', in S. Brown and A. Glasner (eds) *Assessment Matters in Higher Education: Choosing and Using Diverse Approaches*. Buckingham: Open University Press.

Higgins, R., Hartley, P. and Skelton, A. (2002) 'The conscientious consumer: reconsidering the role of assessment feedback in student learning', *Studies in Higher Education* 27(1): 53–64.

Johnston, V. (2001) *Developing Strategies to Improve Student Retention. Reflections from the Work of Napier University's Student Retention Project*. Cambridge: SRHE.

Knight, P.T. (2002) *Being a Teacher in Higher Education*. Maidenhead: Open University Press.

QAA (2006a) Code of Practice for the Assurance of Academic Quality and Standards in Higher Education: Section 6 (accessed 27 October 2008 at http://www.qaa.ac.uk/academicinfrastructure/codeOfPractice/section6).

QAA (2006b) Code of Practice for the Assurance of Academic Quality and Standards in Higher Education: Section 7: p. 5 (accessed 27 October 2008 at http://www.qaa.ac.uk/academicinfrastructure/codeOfPractice/section7).

Romainville, M. and Noel, B. (1998) 'Learning support for first-year university students', *Higher Education Management* 10(2).

Rust, C. (2002) 'The impact of assessment on student learning', *Active Learning in Higher Education* 3: 145–158.

Sellers, J. and Van der Velden, G. (2003) *Supporting Student Retention*. York: LTSN.

Stenhouse, L. (1975) *An Introduction to Curriculum Research and Development*. London: Heinemann Educational.

Taylor, J.A. and Bedford, T. (2004) 'Staff perceptions of factors related to non-completion in higher education', *Studies in Higher Education* 29(3): 375–394.

Yorke, M. (2007) 'Assessment, especially in the first year of higher education: old principles in new wrapping?' From the REAP International Online Conference on Assessment Design for Learner Responsibility, 29–31 May 2007 (available at http://www.reap.ac.uk/reap07, accessed 28 October 2008).

Bibliography

The following are additional texts that provide relevant advice for improving your teaching, using a direct and practical approach.

Kember, D. with McNaught, C. (2007) *Enhancing University Teaching: Lessons from Research into Award-winning Teachers*. London: Routledge.

Morss, K. and Murray, R. (2005) *Teaching at University: A Guide for Postgraduates and Researchers*. London: Sage.

Race, P. (2007) *The Lecturer's Toolkit: A Practical Guide to Assessment, Learning and Teaching* (3rd edn). London: Routledge.

The following are additional texts for helping you to design your assessments.

Bryan, C. and Clegg, K. (eds) (2006) *Innovative Assessment in Higher Education*. Abingdon: Routledge.

Gibbs, G. and Simpson, C. (2005) 'Conditions under which assessment supports students' learning', *Learning and Teaching in Higher Education*, 1: 3–31.

Yorke, M., Bridges, P. and Woolf, H. (2000) 'Mark distributions and marking practices in UK higher education: some challenging issues', *Active Learning in Higher Education* 1(1): 7–27.

Index

(A separate Index follows which lists all the Skills and Super-Skills addressed in the text)

Index of Skills